THE
ECONOMY
OF GOD

DAVID D. SWANSON

THE ECONOMY OF GOD

DISCOVERING THE JOY
OF FINANCIAL OBEDIENCE

The Economy of God:
Discovering the Joy of Financial Obedience
by David D. Swanson

© Copyright 2019
SAINT PAUL PRESS, DALLAS, TEXAS

First Printing, 2019.

All rights reserved. No part of this publication may be reproduced, stored in a retrieval system, or transmitted in any form or by any means, electronic, mechanical, photocopying, recording, or otherwise, without the prior permission of the copyright owner, except for brief quotations included in a review of the book.

ISBN: 9781793135612

Printed in the U.S.A.

*This book is dedicated to
the saints of First Presbyterian Church of Orlando.*

I have been privileged to serve you for nearly 15 years.

You were the first to hear these words and many others, and you have loved me in spite of my very broken, sinful nature. It is your generosity and the generosity of many generations that came before you that helped form the bedrock truths of this book.

I love you and thank God for you.

CONTENTS

Introduction — 9

1. The Impact of Economics — 13
2. Mine or Yours? — 27
3. Plastic Slavery — 41
4. Ready, Shoot, Aim — 57
5. A Dying Breed — 73
6. The Paradox of Giving — 87
7. What About That Rainy Day? — 105
8. Prosperity Perspective — 119
9. Look Up! — 133
10. Time for the Talent Show — 145
11. The Kings and Queens of Planet Earth — 157
12. Protect this House — 171

INTRODUCTION

I am always amazed at how God chooses to work in our lives and the timing by which he reveals things. This book is the result of one of those mysterious revelations. I have been a local church pastor for 27 years, and I have seen time and again how money can become the source of pain, strife, discontent and division. Paul reminds us in 1 Timothy 6:10 that the "love of money" can "pierce us with many griefs." I love the word "pierce." It seems appropriate for what money can do to people. It pierces us. It pains us, *but it does not have to.* Money, when rightly and Biblically understood, can be an absolute source of joy and delight. As I often say to my congregation, it's not what I want from you when I talk about money; it's what I want FOR you. I want you, the reader, to know the joy and delight that is possible when money is rightly yielded to God's discretion.

It was that deep desire in me, during the spring of 2008, that led to this book. I was away on a two-week study leave doing my best to listen to God about what I would preach in the coming year at First Presbyterian Church of Orlando. I had read a few things on stewardship and generosity, but then God gave me an idea that became a twelve week sermon series. It's not just about money, but in Scripture, God has an entire economy that he wants us to observe—a way of working and producing—a way of earning, spending, saving and giving. Naturally, I thought to myself, "Can I actually get away with preaching on the topic of 'money' for twelve weeks? Will the church rebel?" I decided to give it a whirl, and they did not rebel.

In the providence of God, I planned that series before our country plunged into the deepest recession since the Great Depression. We were also right in the middle of a $15 million dollar capital campaign to retire a debt that had crushed much of our ministry capability. Instead of being caught off guard or blindsided, there I was with an entire series devoted to what everyone was wrestling with in their personal lives. It was a gift of God in His perfect time, and the outcome was transcendent. During that season, in the middle of the recession, our giving rose 27% and we raised $13 million of the $15 million for our capital campaign. I have never seen anything like it. People here got very serious about living out of God's economy.

Now, lest you think that everything has been sunshine and roses since, that is not the case. While our giving rose during that sermon series, it did not stay at that 27% level. Thankfully, it hovered in the 8% range and has continued to grow in recent years. However, what I have learned is that it must be spoken about, taught, and preached consistently. As human beings, unless we are reminded, we revert to our "default settings." We are always going to choose self over God. Just as Jesus spoke more about money than any other single subject, we need to be preaching and teaching on money frequently.

Why? Our money is the last bastion of our sinful desires. Martin Luther said that every Christian will go through three levels of conversion: heart, head, and will. The first two are interchangeable in order, but the last one will always be the last one. Our will always gets converted last. It is that moment when our hearts finally say, "OK, Lord. I believe you even to the point that I now yield my will to your will. I want what you want." When we say that, we will begin to yield our money to the Lord. However, what happens in most Christian circles? We never talk about it. We will talk about our health, our marital issues, our children's struggles, and our job issues—everything—but we will never share about our financial position. When is the last time someone told you how much they make? We'll talk about what a great deal we got on a house or a car, but we never say what the price was. We talk in percentages, but not actual amounts. The reason we do this is because as long as no one knows what I make, then I can spend it according to my whims without any accountability. I may yield everything else in my life, but as long as no one knows what I make, I can keep that under my own control. I can keep building my kingdom as I see fit.

That is a recipe for disaster. The best thing I ever did in

this regard was with a small group of men that met once a week. There were four of us, and we decided that we would lay out our complete financial situation in order to build accountability in the one area of life where we lacked it. Over four weeks, we each shared our income, our giving, our saving, our investments and our debt. We agreed that any major expenditure would come to the group for discussion. It was just the check I needed to reign in some bad habits and get my finances back to a place of obedience. Think about doing that in your own life. The reason 94% of those who self-identify as Bible-believing Christians do not tithe is because we have no accountability. Take one or two people into your confidence and talk about this very important dynamic in life.

Finally, as you read this book, it is the compilation of that sermon series, so some references or allusions will seem out of date or place. That is the reason. My prayer is that this will help you once again realize God's economy and that your heart will grow in its desire to live within it.

David Swanson
Winter, 2019

CHAPTER 1

THE IMPACT OF ECONOMICS

"Whoever can be trusted with very little can also be trusted with much..." (Luke 16:10)

"Too many people spend money they earned... to buy things they don't want... to impress people that they don't like." (Will Rogers)

You have likely heard people returning from vacation jokingly say, but with a hint of seriousness, "Boy, I need to take a vacation to recover from this vacation." Clearly, there is some truth to that statement. Every January, I encounter many people who are still recovering from the Christmas/New Year holiday season. They've hurried to visit family and friends or they have been visited by family and friends. Regardless, they're whipped. Yes, these "little" holiday gatherings can often be quite stressful, and that was especially true for us when our kids were little and my parents had just moved into a new house. They had never had a new house before—a home that had been built exactly as they wanted it, so it was a big deal to them, but it was not exactly what I would call a "child-friendly" home. As a young parent, I thought it looked more like a museum. The carpet was lush and lightly colored, the walls were stuccoed and freshly painted, fragile knickknacks adorned almost every surface with nice lamps on every table, and there was artwork on the walls. It was beautiful, and for our family, extremely hazardous.

Our kids were four, three, and one, so when they arrived anywhere, it was like a small tornado. Thus, Leigh and I spent most of our time trying to stand guard over my parent's new home, constantly saying, "Don't touch the walls!" "Don't stand on the sofa!" "Don't bang the china cabinet!" "Don't hang from the lamp shade!" It was exhausting, but even in our vigilance, the house still got damaged. One of our kids had taken a truck and run it up and down one of the nice white walls, leaving a large black streak. Another had managed to put a tear in the carpet going up the stairs, and still another had managed to break the lead glass in the pane on the new front door.

Naturally, my parents were upset. Their new house was damaged. I was upset that my kids had failed to obey my warnings, but none of that resolved who was going to pay for all the damage. Can you say, "Awkward"? The bill was several thousand dollars, and we simply didn't have that kind of money. I made a half-hearted attempt to say we would pay it off in installments, but my parents graciously and kindly wound up paying the bill. Even so, it felt weird after that every time we went to visit. I felt bad. I felt guilty, and while I knew they understood, I knew they were not happy about being out that much money, so the result was relational tension.

Now, call me crazy, but I have learned something very important over the years and it's this: Money affects relationships. My parents and I had an issue over money and it affected our relationship. I know you are astounded by the breadth of my intelligence in making such an assertion, but my bet is that you have already experienced this in some form. Money affects relationships. Corollary A to this truth is also applicable here: How you spend or use the material things that belong to others also affects relationships. My sons now go into my closet to wear my shirts and ties, and when those items wind up back in my closet, wrinkled and wadded up on the floor, it affects my relationship with them.

If someone borrows something of yours that you value, but they abuse it, your relationship is affected. Why do you suppose when the CEO's of the big three automakers went before Congress asking for $30 billion dollars, they were met with a few questions, many of them quite pointed? They were asking for something that belonged to United States taxpayers, and some in Congress were not sure they were going to spend it appropriately. It created tension in their relationship. At the end of 2009, John Thain, CEO of Merrill Lynch, asked his board for a $10 million bonus in the midst of the greatest economic collapse of our time. The *Wall Street Journal* said that the relationship between Thain and the board had become tense as a result. Not exactly groundbreaking reporting. Of course there was tension. Money affects relationships. Have you checked your marriage lately? Money is one of the biggest reasons couples struggle. It's true, isn't it? We all know it is. Money and material things affect relationships.

So, if that's true in our material, human world, then we must understand that it also has enormous application and impact on our spiritual lives—on the nature of our relationship with God. If it's true in our relationship with others, is it not also true in our relationship with God? Of course it is. Money affects our relationship with Him. How we use the things He gives us affects our relationship with Him. In the same way we know it is true in this material world, we know this is true in our relationship with God. Even so, let's be honest: we don't want to think about it. We want to compartmentalize our finances in a separate area from how we relate to God. We like to keep them over in a place we control, but in the back of our mind, we have to know that doing that is going to have an effect on how we relate to God.

As we begin to study this dynamic, there is another foundational truth that we need to make clear: God owns everything. God is the Creator of the universe. It wasn't chance or fate that spun the stars into the heavens or caused the seas to stop at the shoreline. God did it. God created it. As such, it stands to reason that anything we have in this life flows from His hands. Where else could it come from? If God created all things and is at work in all things and governs all things, then anything you have, large or small, has landed in your lap because of God. James 1:17 says, *"Every good and perfect gift is from above."* What we have comes from God. He's the owner. I realize that can be counterintuitive because we feel like we are the ones who earned the money. We got up every morning. We logged the hours and paid the emotional price. We had the ideas and brought them to fruition. We worked the networks and met with the customers, so when the check rolls in, we very much feel like it's ours. It belongs to us, but think about that for a moment. Who gave you the mind that created the idea? Who gave you the gifts to excel in your trade or business? Who provided you the physical strength to endure late nights and early mornings? You didn't give yourself all those things. God did. Therefore, it would make no sense to pat ourselves on the back for something we had no part in creating. God said in Genesis 1:27, "Be fruitful and multiply, fill the earth and subdue it." He created us to take from what He made and bring order out of it. We were called to creat cultures and societies that point back to the glory of the Creator, but it all flows from His hand. The materials we work with and the personal gifts we possess are all from Him. So, if it's all His stuff, then how we use it, how we spend it, and our attitude towards it affects our relationship with God. How could it not? Economics always makes an impact on relationships, and it is certainly true in our relationship with God. We have to start from that premise.

It is that idea that brings me to Luke 16. It is a parable that Jesus told that sounds a bit odd at first reading and thus is one that is often misunderstood. It appears that there is this manager who has done a poor job, and then to cover himself after he gets fired, he starts giving away more of his master's wealth by cutting people's debts. Don't you wish you would run into someone like this in your life? "Hi, your bill is $1000. Oh, just make it $500 and we'll call it even." See how that would work at your local bank. However, that's not the moral of the story. Jesus is not trying to say, "The key to success in business is to be dishonest with your employer's things." That's not it. What Jesus is communicating is a foundation for generosity. He is saying that when it comes to how you live and how you interact with others, generosity should be the place from which we begin because that will affect how we are treated later.

John Calvin writes, "The leading object of this parable is to show that we ought to deal kindly and generously with our neighbors. Christ does not advise us to unfaithful administration, but as all the blessings which God confers upon us are committed to our administration, our Lord now lays down a method of procedure, which will protect us against being treated with rigor." (**Commentaries on the Harmony of the Gospels**, Volume 2) In other words, money affects relationships. If we expect the Lord to be generous with us, don't you think He expects us to treat others with that same generosity? You bet He does. So, in light of this, let's look at this text and see what we can learn about the impact of economics and how we can grow into a more healthy relationship with God.

Christians Are Unprepared to Deal With God's Economy

First, I don't know how to say this without sounding fairly blunt, so here goes: Most of the time, Christians are simply *unprepared to deal with this*. We are not ready, and our relationship with God is never going to get much better until we are able to look at this honestly. Look at the second half of verse 8. It says, "*For the people of this world are more shrewd in dealing with their own kind than are the people of the light.*" Here's what He's saying: We are often more shrewd, more focused, more aware, more prepared in dealing with how our money affects our relationships down here than we are in dealing with how our money affects our relationship with God. With our economy in the place that it's in, have you ever seen so much attention given to how we are spending money in this world? No. The brightest minds are all working hard to figure out the smartest, wisest way to get our worldly economy back on track. How much time, comparatively, do we spend on how our money impacts our relationship with God and with His Body, the Church, the "people of light?"

Alfred Plummer writes, "Worldly people are very farsighted and ready in their transactions with one another for temporal (worldly) objects. The spiritually-minded ought to be equally ready in making one another promote heavenly objects." (***The Pastoral Epistles***, page 171.) In other words, we are very concerned about our horizontal relationships and how money is affecting them, but we should be equally, if not more, concerned about our vertical relationship with God and how it is being impacted by our things. That is the whole purpose of this study. We are spending so much time thinking about the economy of this world, but no one is thinking about the economy of God, when in the end, God says, that is the only economy that matters. We need to prepare ourselves to understand an entirely new economic system, and that's what I aim to do in this book.

Economics Forces You to Consider Your Priorities

Second, when you begin to consider the Economy of God, you will find that *economics forces you to consider your priorities*. I think that was one of the great blessings of the financial crisis/recession that took place in 2008-10. Many people had to re-evaluate their priorities in light of having less. Many were forced to ask: "What really matters?" You've no doubt heard this before, but Jesus says in verse 13, *"No servant can serve two masters. Either he will hate the one and love the other, or he will be devoted to the one and despise the other. You cannot serve both God and money."*

Please understand what I am <u>not</u> saying here. I am not trying to downplay the importance or significance of money in our lives. When you are out of a job and trying to figure out how to pay your bills and stay in your house, money is VERY important. However, we have to be clear that money is not THE most important thing. When we consider our current economic situation in light of what God has said, it forces us to think about what's important. It forces us to ask the question, "Who am I serving? Am I serving the goddess of materialism and personal comfort, or am I serving the living God who has given me all things? Am I being faithful to Him in what He has given to me?"

In my personal life and in my ministry, I have always found it interesting how God makes this truth plain in our lives. It really does not take much for us to see what's important with clarity. A successful doctor, a man who has everything that a person could possibly want, walks in the daily pain of divorce and the added suffering of taking his teenage son to rehab for the second time. He sits in his waterside mansion with three luxury cars in the garage, and he says, "I would trade all of this to have my family back." He has become acutely aware of what his priorities actually are, though he had not chosen to live according to those priorities up to that point. He does today, but God's economics didn't become evident until that moment.

One Thanksgiving, I took my family down to the county jail to lead a Thanksgiving worship service for the inmates, and I watched as my children engaged a group of inmates in a conversation about what they are thankful for. They exchanged requests for prayer about the personal needs of their lives, and suddenly, whether or not they had a game system or a cell phone or even a car, for that matter, was no longer important. In those moments, things become very clear.

So, let me ask you: Honestly, who do you serve? Who is your master? Without question, some of you feel like you are chained to your master better known as your checkbook or your investment account. You are chained to your mortgage and your bills because you have to be; you have no choice. You have to serve that master because that master is hard. While that may be true, you can start to cut those chains. All of us can begin to reset our priorities away from the economy of this world and toward the economy of God by starting to invest ourselves in what matters, by realigning our priorities, and by making different choices. Yes, you have to work and you have to pay those bills, but those bills will not look the same when you start serving a different master. Those bills will not look the same when you start doing things in your life to be generous and servant-minded with others.

You can also start to make different decisions about how you spend your money. Don't be prideful. If you need to, ask for financial help. I often connect people with Christian financial managers who can help people not only get out of debt, but they also help people plan to give. This goes back to whether or not we're ready. We all have a plan for retirement and for college and for this vacation or for that thing, but do any of us plan our generosity? In the economy of God, we should, because that's our priority. The bottom line is this: In your guts, you know what's important. You know that the almighty God is the one relationship you have that really matters. Our problem is we don't live according to that priority. So, our challenge is to take some time and make some decisions so that it does not take a tragic event to show us what's important but that we would begin to live according to Godly priorities even now.

True Wealth

Third, when we start to live according to the Economy of God, we are forced to define *true wealth*. Look at verse 9. Jesus says, "*. . . so that, when it is gone, you will be welcomed into eternal dwellings.*" He says we need to use our worldly wealth to invest in an eternal Kingdom because one day, our worldly wealth will be gone, and then what will we be left with? You can't take this world's wealth with you. We know that. Even so, heavenly wealth does not seem real to us. It does not really seem to apply to our lives today. Right now, all of us dread that monthly statement we get that tells us the dwindling amount of our worldly wealth. However, we don't get a statement from Heaven, do we? Wouldn't it be great if at the same time, we got a statement from heaven that said, "Your heavenly, eternal wealth is way up this month!" It might make us look at things down here a bit differently, wouldn't it? It would lead us to focus on what we have there instead of being distracted by what we don't have here, but we don't normally grasp that truth.

Naturally, our failure to grasp it has consequences. If we don't recognize the value of our treasure in heaven, then our worldly wealth often becomes a distraction to us in our relationship with God. Remember, money affects relationships. Therefore, as Christianity plays out around the world, I see an interesting phenomenon that Americans miss. The poor walk more closely with the Lord than the wealthy comparatively. I see this over and over again as our church members go on mission trips to different places in the world. They return having encountered deep poverty, but exclaim, "They had nothing and yet they were so content and joyful in the Lord!" The poor are not distracted by what they don't have. They know they can't provide for themselves so they trust more deeply in the things of God and they invest in what gives eternal wealth. In America, we have so much that we get lulled into thinking that we can provide for ourselves. We don't have a deep acute need for God. Why would we? We already have so much, God feels like some sort of unnecessary add on. We become so caught up in what we have or what we've lost that we scarcely have the time to think about the things of God, which is exactly why God says to us, "You need to redefine truth wealth. It's NOT what you have here. What you have here does not last. Start investing in something else."

Matthew Henry writes, "The riches of this world are the less; grace and glory are the greater . . . He that serves God and does good with his money will serve God and do good with the more noble and valuable talents of wisdom and grace, and spiritual gifts; but he that buries the one talent of this world's wealth will never improve the five talents of spiritual riches. God withholds his grace from covetous worldly people more than we are aware of . . . (if we act that way), how can we expect to be entrusted with spiritual riches?" (**Matthew Henry Commentary on Luke**, chapter 16).

In at least some way, the economy of God is built on trust. Why would God entrust to me the deep spiritual riches of an abiding relationship with Him if I am not trustworthy in the littlest things He gives me in this life? If I am not able to handle the paltry wealth of this world, why would He entrust to me the greater riches of His Kingdom? You see, money affects relationships. It affects how God reveals Himself to you more than you realize. Paul prayed in Ephesians 1:18, "*I pray that you may know the riches of his glorious inheritance with all the saints.*" In other words, I pray that you will understand true wealth. It's not here; it's in another Kingdom. May we learn to be faithful in what we have here so that God will trust us with the greater riches—the true wealth—of who He is.

I believe with every fiber of my being that the Economy of God has far more to help the world than solving the economy of this world. I believe that what we have said is more critical than anything the *Wall Street Journal* tells us, but the world doesn't see it that way. If we live this, make no mistake, we will get the sneer. The same sneer the Pharisees gave to Jesus will be given to us because very few understand the Economy of God, but I tell you today, it is the most important thing for us and for our church.

Dallas Willard wrote, "The greatest issue facing the world today, with all its heart-breaking needs, is whether those who are identified as Christians will become disciples – students, apprentices, practitioners – of Jesus Christ, steadily learning from Him how to live the life of the Kingdom of Heaven in every corner of human existence. Will they break out of the churches to be His Church – to be, without human force or violence, His mighty force for good on earth, drawing the churches after them toward the eternal purposes of God?" (***The Great Omission: Reclaiming Jesus's Essential Teachings on Discipleship***, page 176) Will we? May we learn to live the life of the Kingdom of Heaven—the Economy of God—in every corner of our human existence such that our relationship with Him grows and deepens, giving us the riches of God.

CHAPTER 2

MINE OR YOURS?

"Every good and perfect gift is from above, coming down from the Father of the heavenly lights, who does not change like shifting shadows." (James 1:17)

"Money is not the most important thing in the world. Love is. Fortunately, I love money." (Jackie Mason)

I want to begin this chapter by asking you a question: What do you think your life is worth? In this season of economic uncertainty, a lot of us have been calculating our declining net worth, but the question goes far deeper than that. For that reason, I was struck by a story I found not long ago about a young Australian man named Ian Usher. Mr. Usher, 44, decided that he was going to sell his entire life on EBay. He had recently been through a painful divorce from his wife and had come to the conclusion that he could not live in their house or be with their friends. The memories were just too painful. He convinced his boss to let whoever bought his life have his job for two weeks, after which the boss could decide whether or not to keep the person. Then there was all the equipment that goes hand-in-hand with Ian's outdoor, adventurous lifestyle: kite-surfing gear, bodyboards, a mountain bike, and a skydiving outfit. He convinced his friends to befriend whoever the person was. His house, his car, the furniture – it was all included. He got all the elements of his life together and put it up for auction. The morning it went online, the bidding started at $1. This is only slightly more than I would receive should I decide to auction my life; however, it got better. By 3 p.m., the bidding had passed $400,000, and by 6 p.m. there were one hundred bidders with the high bid reaching $1.8 million. Now, if you go to his website, you can't really find out what happened after that unless you want to pay $2.95 to subscribe to a host of other things.

    Mr. Usher turned into a money-making machine, but the whole thing raises some interesting questions for us: How much is our life worth? But even beyond that, who owns my life and all that I have? Mr. Usher decided he was going to sell his life, but that presumed that he was its rightful owner. I remember when I was little I tried to sell my sister's bike to one of my friends and he said, "That's not even your bike." I said, "That's okay. She won't care." Obviously, she did. What, in this life, really belongs to us? Do we own our stuff? Do we own our life? Or is it possible that someone else does? Is it possible, as the Bible says, that someone else has purchased my life by His blood or that someone else is the source, the owner, of all I have?

I share that because I think it highlights for us the interesting way we treat things in life. We are big believers in ownership. We want to acquire things for ourselves because what we have is a sign of our success or our worth. And that's what has gotten a lot of people in trouble. We can't afford a beach house, but by golly, I have to look as good as this person or that person, so I'm going to go in debt up to my eyeballs to get it. Correspondingly, if I *don't* own something, then I'm not going to value it as much nor will I treat it as well as if I'd been the owner. Do you ever notice how awful some bathrooms can be in airports or schools or public buildings? People treat those spaces poorly because they don't care about them. It's not their building. They don't know the owner, so why should they care? In many respects, I think this attitude is very much why giving in our culture has grown more and more shallow. We only care about what belongs to us and the rest is simply not our concern.

In the last twenty-five years as our society has gotten wealthier, we actually have given less on a percentage basis. World Vision has done some interesting study on generosity in America. Do you know who the largest givers are in the United States? People who earn less than $10,000 a year; they give away on average 5.2% of their income. Do you know who gives the least? People who make more than $100,000; they give away on average only 1.6% of their income. Further, as you look at America since 1950, our average charitable giving has dropped from 3.4% to 2.6%. Think about the explosion of our economy over those decades. We have more now than we've ever had in our history and yet we give less. It makes no sense, but then again, maybe it does. I think we have gotten more and more confused about ownership. The things we think we own, we take care of; but if we don't own it, if it doesn't belong to us and we don't know who the owner is then why should we care? Why should we invest in anything beyond ourselves? In an individualistic world, what's beyond "me" doesn't matter, so I will have no motivation towards generosity.

It's that idea that brings me to an important text in **1 Chronicles 29**. The Israelites are bringing an offering to the Lord, and I think it is important for us to note how that happened. The Bible says they brought it with "wholehearted devotion," and hopefully, not only will we understand why they gave in such a manner, but we'll learn to give in that fashion as well. Historically, Israel was on the brink of the most significant change in leadership that she had ever had. David had been king for almost forty years and during that time, for the most part, Israel had prospered. God had blessed her. Yet now, David is about to depart and his son Solomon is going to be king. So, if you were David, you can certainly understand why you might be concerned about Israel's future. You have worked hard to draw them to the Lord, to remind them of their calling to be witnesses to the world of the one, true and living God, and yet, you also know there's a history of Israel's failure in that regard. You know that whenever Israel had prospered in the past, she had a tendency to become prideful and to value worldly things. She had an inclination to worship material things rather than the things of God. That whole golden calf experiment jumps to mind as an example. So, what does David do?

David wants one last shot. Before he leaves, he wants to give one final message to the God's people in order to remind them of their foundation. God is God and there is no other. God is the One to be trusted and obeyed. So, what does he do? He calls the people together in worship. He calls them together in the presence of the Lord. It is quite similar to what happens in churches all over the world every Sunday. Verse one says David gathered the whole assembly together, and when he does, what does he start talking about? Interestingly, he starts talking about money. Giving. Generosity. Before he even prays, he launches into why the people should give. I can assure you this is not what you get taught in preaching class during seminary. Talking about money as your lead subject is going to alienate your hearers and make them restless, but David does it nonetheless.

It is a curious and yet highly strategic move, so why do you suppose he does that? Pulling back and looking at the entire Biblical arc, we find something similar at work. Over the entire ministry of Jesus, money is the most frequently discussed subject. Think about that. If pastors are charged with presenting to their congregations the breadth of the Biblical witness, and money is the most frequent subject, then it stands to reason that money should be our most frequently mentioned topic, but it's not. If it were, you and I both know what would happen. Mutiny! Tom Ehrich wrote an article in *USA Today* about the materialism of our age. It was entitled "**Not Heard From the Pulpit**." He said, "Jesus devoted roughly two-thirds of His teachings to our need to give away wealth and to value humility and servanthood more than power. Yet, in a typical congregation, it is safer to preach about someone else's sexual behavior than about the wise and faithful use of money." As much as I hate to admit it, it's true. Ehrich is right.

When I first started talking to the staff about doing this series, do you know what came up again and again? Attendance. Our staff and elders said if you do a ten to fifteen week series on money, people will stop coming because they'll think we're after theirs. Money is not what they want to talk about. It's too personal. Don't do it. Thankfully, that didn't stop me, but at a certain level, they're right. We don't like it when the church talks to us about our money, even though it's the subject that Jesus talked about the most. Shouldn't you have an expectation of me as your pastor to speak often on the subject that Jesus spoke most often about? I think so, but as I said, I don't and for good reason. We're not there yet, but I hope we will be soon. If Jesus spent more time teaching about money than any other subject, would you not then assume that God thinks it is one of our biggest problems—one of our biggest struggles? You bet.

Money and materialism have a powerful influence on our life, and if we are not careful, their influence will lead us away from God. I preach on this not because I want to annoy you. I preach on it because I know we need to find freedom from the power money wields, and one of the primary places we find that freedom is in worship. David knew it, so he calls the people to worship, and in his final message, he immediately addresses the offering of their material wealth. From David's final message to the Israelites, what do we learn about our material resources and the way we worship God through our giving?

You Don't Own Your Life and You Don't Own Your Stuff

First, as hard as this may be to digest, *you don't own your life and you don't own your stuff*. God does. God is the owner. I've said this to you before on several occasions, but I subscribe to the theory of communication that says, tell them what you're going to tell them, tell them, then tell them what you told them. I say it again because it's a tough concept and one that, were we to adopt it and believe it, may mean an adjustment in our lives or our lifestyle to actually become obedient before the Lord. Even so, our obedience to the Lord in the area of money becomes much easier when we realize one thing: We don't own it to begin with. Our things are not actually ours. I know that flies in the face of everything your bank or your boss is trying to tell you, but what does David say in verses 11 and 12? "*Yours,*

O Lord, is the greatness and the power and the glory and the majesty and the splendor, for everything in heaven and earth is yours . . . wealth and honor come from you, you are the ruler of all things."

Now, I know we can give an approving nod to that, but in our heart, do we really believe it? This is where our theology becomes very important. What we believe actually trickles down to how we understand what we have. If we believe God is the creator of the universe, then all things flow from His hand. That's why David said *"yours is the greatness and the power and the glory and the majesty."* Further, if we believe our ultimate purpose is to be about what He's about, that the reason God created us to begin with was to worship and glorify Him, then it makes perfect sense that He would intend for us to use what He has entrusted to us for His purposes. This is the process of our spiritual maturity. When we come to believe that not only is Jesus Christ Savior and Lord to us, but that He is also the singular hope of the world, then everything changes. If we believe that Jesus Christ is the hope the world yearns for, then giving to the cause of Christ and the extension of His Kingdom will become the priority of our giving. Yes, there are many wonderful charities that we can give to and we should, however, they are not first because they are not eternal. We begin by bringing our "firstfruits" to the Lord, and that, of course, has implications for the rest of our lives.

I think it brings us back to our original question: What is our life worth, and who actually owns it? Do we value the building of our own kingdoms, believing that we are the lords and owners therein? Do we value the building of our kingdoms such that we invest only in those things? Or have we become convinced by the hope of the Gospel that reveals to us the One who is the true and rightful owner of all things? And having seen the state of our world, are we willing to yield the lordship of our life and the ownership of our things so that they can be used for His purposes?

I once stumbled across a piece of artwork, a sculpture, entitled *Self Made Man*. It was funded by an arts group called Funding Freedom which said of the sculpture, "The powerful image of the rugged 'Self-Made Man' chiseling himself out of a solid block of rock captures the essence of the freedom philosophy – that left to his own devices, man will use his God-given talents to be creative, productive, and prosperous. Using free will, he will better his own situation and that of those around him, thereby influencing in a positive way his own destiny."

As a child, I heard that term a lot—self-made man—because my father was one. He grew up in relative poverty on Long island, New York. He managed to get to Dartmouth College and SMU law school and build a successful law practice. Many who stood by watching would have said my father made himself, but I can assure you that's not what he would tell you. He would tell you that it was by the grace of God that generous people along the way put him in the right places and paid the bills and helped get the scholarships that got him to what he became. He would tell you it was God's gracious hand that provided all along the way. As such, to this day, my father is one of the most generous men I know.

Compare that to the sculpture. I ask you, with all due respect to the artist and the foundation, can a sculpture chisel itself out of rock? When I read that statement, I had to laugh a bit. Of course a sculpture can't sculpt itself, and we are no more responsible for what we have than a sculpture is for its own existence. We depend wholly on the hands of our Maker, the One who has set our life in motion and who has promised to provide for us. Even so, there are still many of us, hammer and chisel in hand, who believe we are forming our own lives out of the rock. Here's the thing: Your ability to grasp the fallacy of that will determine your future slavery or freedom in regard to your money, your stuff and your things. If you don't get that, you will always have a foundation of rock around your feet, binding you and keeping you there, but if you do grasp the truth of God, then God can set you free. You won't be a slave to your money because it doesn't all depend on you. You are not the sole source of provision. Your identity is not in what you have. You are only the steward of what God gives. The task becomes discerning how God wants you to use those resources, and thankfully, He has made that pretty clear.

Growing Towards Faithful Giving

Second, I believe *the more convinced we become of who God is the more faithful we will become in our giving.* As we grasp the wondrous assignment given the church to go into all the world and make disciples, the more sacrificial we will become in our giving. We will know that there can be no greater offering we can make than to give generously to the work of God in the world. Our wealth, our money, is to be devoted and given according to God's purposes—the purposes of building His Kingdom. If that is true, then financial decisions become spiritual ones. Therein lays the seminal truth: Giving is not actually a financial decision. In God's economy, giving is a spiritual decision. Therefore, I need to consult the Owner on how I'm spending His money.

I'll never forget when John David was little and we went to a baseball game. I gave him a $50 bill to go get some food and he came back with no change. I said, "What happened?" He said, "Oh, nothing. I just told the lady to keep it. She tried to give it back, but I just said 'Nah, don't worry about it.'" He obviously had not consulted me about how he was spending my money. The same is true for us. How faithfully do we do that? Again, our practice will be determined by what we believe about ownership.

As we grow in this and become more faithful in our finances, God extends the hope of the Gospel. People need the truth which you have in your hearts, the truth that has redeemed you. Research reported in a *USA Today* article has shown that, in the state of Washington, 25% of the people have no faith at all. There are eight other states just like it. One quarter of the people have no faith. The task is great. We've seen two more incidents of violence in our schools by adults and students alike; two more incidents of sexual abuse by adults upon our students in this community. There is a growing conflict between Christianity and Islam. The task is great, and it leaves us feeling overwhelmed.

Even so, I would say that our task is no greater than what faced Solomon. It is no greater than the task of the Israelites in their world. And just like building the temple, building an effective ministry for the glory of Christ and the transformation of the world is costly; it's expensive, and it requires our faithful giving. Richard Foster wrote, "When we let go of money we are letting go of part of ourselves and part of our security. But this is precisely why it is important to do it. It is one way to obey Jesus' command to deny ourselves. When we give money, we are releasing a little more of our egocentric selves and a little more of our false security. Giving frees us to care." (**Money, Sex and Power**, page 83)

From the very beginning, the reason God calls us to give, calls us to understand ownership, is to help care for others. Again from World Vision, we learn that this concept of tithing actually works. Right now, the current cost of providing for the worldwide basic human needs of food, clean water and shelter is $1.8 billion dollars. If just Christians in America tithed, it would raise an additional $2.6 billion. We could meet the need and have $800 million left over for worldwide evangelism. If we were just obedient in our generosity, we would not need governments to take care of every issue, and in the process WE would be the ones to receive the larger blessing. There is good in it for us because we learn the lessons of life and humility and security that we can learn no other way. That's what David was talking about. That's what this is about. It's not about an institution. It's not about the church as an organization. It's not about me or you. It is about the Lord, the giver of life. It is about the great task of sharing His life with others. I think we're doing that. I think we're starting to make a difference in our community and in our world and that difference is fueled by your generosity.

However, make no mistake about it, we can choose to own our stuff. We can stubbornly resist what God has revealed, but there is a cost for that. It costs nothing to reach no one. It costs nothing to create nothing. It costs nothing to keep the message of Christ's love contained only in these four walls. It costs nothing to keep our missionaries home. It costs nothing to keep the students in our urban neighborhoods out of our church. It costs nothing to staff empty classrooms. Churches are dying because they do not preach the sacrifice of Christ and they do not preach the costly nature of extending His life to the world. They do not preach faithful stewardship and the Biblical imperative of God's ownership. Well, risky as it may be, we do. I do. It is essential for our growth. It is essential for our life. It is essential for His life to be extended to our community and beyond.

I can talk or write about it all day, but it ultimately comes down to you. Generosity is one of those things that you'll never fully understand until you lean into it and do it. You have to decide. I don't know where I read this, but it has stuck with me. Someone said, "Be who you say you are." I think about that a lot. I want to be who I say I am, and that involves every aspect of my life. I pray that we would do that. Are we 'self-made,' believing that by the sheer force of our will we can chisel our own life out of solid rock, its beauty and blessing being shaped by our own hand? Or do we sense that Someone else, all along, has been shaping, molding, and providing for us in a manner we could never comprehend? You're not self-made; you're God-made. Your life is His life, not to sell or own casually because it fits your whim or need, but to be given to Him in humble thanks.

CHAPTER 3

PLASTIC SLAVERY

"Keep your lives free from the love of money and be content with what you have, because God has said, "Never will I leave you; never will I forsake you." (Hebrews 13:5)

"There is a sufficiency in the world for man's need but not for man's greed." (Mahatma Gandhi)

I want to begin this message by telling you that I live with a lot of debt. I am not necessarily proud of that fact, but I have a lot of personal indebtedness that I have accumulated over time. I am deeply indebted to my parents for providing twenty-two years of food and shelter, especially after I told them in high school that I could make it just fine on my own, thank you very much. I am indebted to my high school basketball coach, Bo

Snowden, who kept me on the team in spite of my triple-threat skills of being slow, weak, and unable to jump. I am indebted to my wife for staying married to me even though I am no fun on Saturday nights and completely unable to fix anything in our home. I am indebted to the state trooper who pulled me over for speeding but let me go with just a "Please slow down." I am deeply indebted to First Presbyterian Church for allowing me to continue as your pastor even though you know these things about me. And, oh yes, I am indebted to my mortgage company for the remaining mortgage on my house. Now, isn't it interesting that out of all the things I've mentioned, I only get a bill from one of those creditors? I owe all of them, but those debts have all been wiped out except that last one. For some reason, my mortgage company has not seen fit to clear my account.

I share that because I want us to take some time to think about the issue of personal indebtedness and the way in which it impacts our lives. I think it's far too easy for us to assume that the only debts we carry are financial ones. That is not true. We are indebted to many people over the course of our lives for what they have given us, and we need to be careful to ensure our gratitude towards those people and to God when those debts are canceled. Yet even with that overall perspective on personal indebtedness, there is no doubt that the debt that impacts our lives the most is the financial kind, and we are feeling that more than ever before.

According to *American Progress*, "America's families are

caught in a perfect storm. Massive amounts of debt, falling home prices, disappearing jobs, flat wages, lower benefits, and skyrocketing costs for the most important consumer items are bringing many families to the edge of financial ruin. Household debt averaged a record 133.7% of disposable income in the fourth quarter of 2007, with families spending 14.3% of their disposable income to service that debt." An online virtual meeting site called MeetUp.Com reports they now have 138 groups who meet online to talk about their debt situations, up from only 24 groups one year ago. Some examples: Michael, a 34-year-old sales manager in St. Louis, drives a silver 5 series BMW sedan, wears $200 jeans and has $25,000 in credit card debt. Shawnda, an accountant in Washington, DC, earning a six-figure income, has a total of $54 in savings. John, a father of four in Dallas, earns $175,000 annually, but has debt on a boat, two pieces of land in Colorado, a condo, and his current home, plus $30,000 in credit card debt. As one church leader said, "Debt is a way of life for us in the United States."

Our chosen way of life is having a huge impact on our larger world, especially as it relates to generosity. Because of our debt, we have nothing to give. An Oxford survey revealed that 25% of Americans who identify themselves as "strong" or "Biblical" Christians give nothing—not one dollar. The average gift was 1.6% of after-tax income, down from 2.3% in the early 1960's. Five percent (5%) of these people give 60% of the total amount given. As Americans have grown more wealthy and more indebted, we have also grown less generous. Rob Moll writes in *Christianity Today*, "A major reason Christians don't give more is because many can't. There's a misperception that if we have this really wealthy church in this well-heeled neighborhood giving should be a slam dunk. Instead, many of the folks in those neighborhoods driving luxury cars and going to their summer cottages are doing it all on credit."

Perhaps you have found a bit of yourself or your situation in what I have said so far. My bet is you have. It's not exactly a stretch in saying that we have a debt problem. That has become painfully obvious, and what has happened in this country in the past twelve months is in large part because of that problem.

It is that idea that brings us to the book of Proverbs to try and understand why we have this problem and what God may have to say about this whole concept of debt. Let me be clear at the beginning: I am not about to give you a formula for how to get out of debt, thought there are wonderful ministries that can help with that, most notably Dave Ramsey's Financial Peace University. I am not going to address every aspect of indebtedness; however, I do hope to show you the roots of the problem and the core Biblical principles in addressing it. God knows us intimately, and He anticipates where we are prone to fall as is written in the book of Proverbs. It's essentially a "how to" book on everyday living. As one commentator said, "It touches on nearly every department of life and shows God's direct interest in it. Wisdom does not consist of the contemplation of abstract principles, but a relationship with

God in concrete situations." In other words, living wisely is not found in some sort of abstract domain, but in the day-to-day application of one's relationship with God into real world situations like money and debt. It doesn't get much more practical than that, does it? So, we come to **Proverbs 22:7** which says, *"The borrower is servant to the lender"* and **Proverbs 3:26** which says, *"The Lord will be your confidence."* In the day-to-day application of our relationship with God, to the real world in which we live, to this issue of debt, what does this teach us?

The Foundation of the Gospel is a Debt-free World

First, we need to recognize that the foundation of the Gospel, meaning the way in which God created us to live and work in relationship to Him, *is a debt-free world*. Going back to **Proverbs 3:25 and 26**, it says, *"Have no fear of sudden disaster or the ruin that overtakes the wicked, for the Lord will be your confidence."* Implied in the text is the foundation of Israel's relationship with God from the very beginning. The wicked are fearful and come to ruin because they live outside of that relationship. The faithful, however, those to whom Solomon is writing, are in relationship with the Lord, and thus, should have confidence. Why? What is that confidence born of? Well, let's go back to the beginning. When God created Adam and Eve and established His relationship with them, He gave them everything. He gave them life; He gave them love; He gave them each other; He gave them food and nourishment; He gave them work and purpose. There was nothing that He did not give them, yet at no time was there ever any word about what they owed God. All this was given to them out of God's love and for their mutual benefit and enjoyment.

The foundation of our walk with God is living debt-free, but obviously that was lost somewhere along the way. We chose to live outside of that relationship and became indebted to the righteousness of God because of our sin. After that, we *did* owe Him. You see, this debt problem started a long time ago. Most people think this is a financial problem. It's not. At its core, debt is a spiritual problem. We want something, something that we feel will make our lives better or our spirits happier, and because we are not being filled by God's love, we go get it when we cannot afford it. We're never content or satisfied, so we look outside of God and become indebted to the things of the world.

Thankfully, God knows us well. He anticipates our resistance to His truth, so He speaks to it again and again. We move to the New Testament, but it's the same truth. The Gospel message tells us that Jesus came to cancel our sin debt. By the cross of Jesus Christ, God showed us once again that His plan, His desire for us is debt-free living. Paul writes in **Ephesians 2:8-9**, "*For it is by grace that you have been saved, through faith and this not from yourselves, it is the gift of God - not by works, so that no one can boast.*" Salvation is a gift. You don't get it and then have to pay it off. It's free, thus, we live in confidence. We don't have to fear the trials of this world because we know God is faithful. We live in confidence because we don't have to worry about doing something to ensure God's provision and faithfulness in our lives. We are confident He is going to take care of us. We get unconditional, debt-free love and care. How good is that? What a contrast to how most of us live today!

Even so, let's remember that while there is no cost to us, there was enormous cost to God. For a debt of any kind to be canceled – a sin debt or a financial debt – the debt must be absorbed. If your bank were to call you and say, "We've canceled your mortgage" that would only be possible if they absorbed the cost. In the same way, God has canceled the debt of our sin only because He absorbed the cost through the sacrificial death of His son. Jesus bore the cost. That is the root of forgiveness in this world. The Lord's Prayer reminds us "forgive us our debts as we forgive our debtors." If God has absorbed the cost of our sin, then we are called to absorb the sin debts of others against us. When my friend wounds me or hurts me in some way, our relationship is reconciled only when I chose to bear the pain – the cost – of that wound and move forward in the relationship. Forgiveness is costly, but it is also freeing. It frees me from living in anger and bitterness towards others as I entrust their lives to God. Forgiveness is actually the gift you give yourself, and it's grounded in the nature of indebtedness. We stand debt-free in regard to sin before God, but we must always take seriously the cost He bore for us. Our lives, in that sense, were "purchased by His blood."

The Result is Personal Slavery

Second, if we fall into the trap of not waiting on or trusting in God to provide, we're in trouble. *The result is personal slavery.* **Proverbs 22:7**: *"The borrower is servant to the lender."* Debt makes us slaves. Our lives begin to be oriented not around what God has provided, but around what we want, and correspondingly, what we owe. And we've all seen people like that, haven't we? People absolutely enslaved by what they have.

The world was astounded when one of the world's most well-known financial managers, Bernie Madoff, was arrested for bilking his clients out of almost $50 billion dollars. He wanted a certain lifestyle that was beyond his reach, so he spent other people's money to get it, creating a false life of spiraling lies and debts he could never cover. He wanted more, more, more, and sadly, he is not alone. We function the same way. We see what others have, and we want it. We think what we have defines us or makes us worthy, thus, if one family has this thing or that thing, then for me to feel as worthy as them, I need to have it, too. It doesn't matter to me whether or not I have the money. I'm going to have it—now; and in turn we become slaves to debt. Before we know it, this thing we thought we needed to have because it would help us feel worthy has become an albatross around our necks that saps our energy, diverts our attention from God, and squelches any desire we might have to be generous with others.

What's amazing, too, is that this is a relatively new

phenomenon in the past fifty years. The first credit card of any significance was not issued until the late 1960's. Up until that time, it did not occur to people to buy things they did not have the money for. If you didn't have enough money to buy a car, you didn't get a car. If you didn't have money for a dress, you didn't buy it. If you bought a house, you put more than half the value down. I was talking to one family about the home their parents had built in the 60's. The father had been a very successful businessman, but he did not build his dream home until he was seventy years old. Why? The money he made went back into the business, and he didn't have enough money to pay for the house until that point in his life. It would never have occurred to him to build it before then. He didn't have the money, so he didn't build.

Our brains have been trained to think the complete opposite. We are trained on instant gratification. If we want something, we don't want to wait. With the advent of new technologies and overnight shipping, we have grown accustomed to the quick satisfaction of our wants. We want it now and we get it fast - which is the opposite of the ethic of the Gospel. God wants us to be enslaved to nothing, to be controlled by nothing, including our wants. Further, part of a Christian ethic is a life of sacrifice and generosity. Living beyond our means enslaved to debt is denying the very manner in which God has loved and cared for us. So, if that's where we've gotten, how do we move from being enslaved back to this idea of debt-free living in relationship to God?

It is Expressed by Our Contentment and Our Obedience

Third, our ability to move out of slavery to debt *is grounded in our relationship with God expressed by our contentment and our obedience.* Let me ask you: Is your identity, your confidence, grounded in the Lord? The more you are able to answer that question positively, the more you will find contentment in the material circumstances of your life. Paul wrote in **Philippians 4:11 and 13**, *"I have learned the secret of being content in any and every situation . . . I can do everything through Him who strengthens me."* What was his secret in finding contentment? His secret was his complete dependence on God. God was sufficient. He may have wanted other things, but he was also content not to have them. I'm not sure that many of us can say the same thing because we lack Paul's understanding; therefore, we are constantly stacking up debts to the world in search of what only God can give us. So, you need to ask yourself: How much is enough? Until we learn to place our hope and confidence in God, we will never have an answer. The answer will always be "more than I have right now" and we will be slaves. Are you content with what you have?

The corresponding question is, "Are you being obedient to what God has said?" Going back to the beginning, isn't our initial debt because we became disobedient? Yes. No human being incurred any debt until he or she starting living outside the bounds of God's law, so part of the answer to our slavery to debt is becoming obedient to what God has said to us about our things. **Deuteronomy 15** describes the early period of God's relationship with Israel. He says in verses 4-6, *"The Lord's time for canceling debts has been proclaimed.* (There it is again: God is always about freeing us from our debts.) *You may require payment from a foreigner, but you must cancel any debt your brother owes you. There should be no poor among you, for in the land the Lord your God is giving you to possess, he will richly bless you,* **if only you fully obey the Lord your God and are careful to follow all these commands. You will lend to many nations but you will borrow from none**."

In the Kingdom of God, our lives are to be oriented not around ourselves but around our community, the needy, and the Lord. When we are obedient to that, we're never going to get ahead of ourselves. We are naturally going to be generous, caring, and outwardly focused. When we are, God makes it pretty clear that He will provide. That may not mean He provides what we think we need, but He will provide, and He is faithful. No doubt, this is where it gets tough. We know we feel that discontent which gets us in trouble, but are we willing to be obedient as a possible solution to that discontent?

This is not easy, and I realize I have been up in your business a little bit. This is one of those messages that leave you squirming in your chairs because I'm poking on a raw spot for all of us. It hits us right where we live, myself included. For some of you, getting out of this slavery may mean a radical readjustment of your lifestyle. If you want to stop being a slave, if you want to once again become free in your finances, free to give and serve the needs of others, then it may mean a radical reorientation of your life. And this is where I'm going to lose many of you. How would you do that? What would other people think? How could you live without this thing or that place? Well, I'm not sure, but I know Jesus did say, *"What does it profit a man if he gains the whole world, but loses his soul?"* (Mark 8:36)

When we lived in Ft. Myers, I coached my boys in little league baseball. One of the families we got to know was the Weyer (*not the actual name) family. Their boys were Tim and Tony, and like my boys John David and Alex, they were brothers playing on our baseball team. They were not star athletes by any means, but they were sweet-spirited, gentle young men. About a year after we came to Orlando, we heard that Tim had contracted an inoperable, malignant brain tumor, but his faith was having a huge impact on the community as a result. During his grueling medical treatment, he prayed fervently and wrote in his journal about his growing faith in God. The Fort Myers High School sophomore became convinced God had a higher purpose for him. He wrote "I honestly believe that one of the reasons I have this tumor is to make a wish and raise money for all the kids in Africa."

That wish gave birth to an outpouring of funds and servants such that an orphanage bearing his name was built, housing sixty children in Kenya. Twenty-five people went over from Ft. Myers to this little village in Kenya to spend two weeks, painting and building and preparing the facility for its opening which took place one day after the first anniversary of Tim's death. However, the amazing thing was one man who went, Joel Tyler, a resident of Naples, Florida earning a six-figure income, did not come back. He stayed. He became the Operations Director of that orphanage because he was so radically changed by the faith of a dying boy and the call God had put on his heart to help the needy children of Africa.

    I am blown away when I see something like that because that man found something that was the greatest value to him. He found something that was more important than any earthly thing. It was his "pearl of great price." He decided to be about what God was about, and he was willing to radically reorient his life to do it; he was willing to trade everything to have it, and my bet is that he is experiencing greater freedom now than he has ever known in his life. I'm not sure many of us could make that same statement. If we want to find that "pearl of great price", we must be willing to closely examine our lives to find where we are placing our confidence and dependence. What is it that gives us our identity? If those things have not led us to true contentment, then we must be willing to change our lives, reorienting them in the direction of Jesus. I know. That's a tall order. It reminds me of the rich young ruler who came to Jesus seeking the meaning of life. When Jesus told him he must sell all his worldly things, Matthew 19:22 says "He went away sad, for he had great wealth." We're just like that man. We struggle mightily to let go of our things and the value we place on them to do for us what only God can do. Will we, based on the hope of the Gospel in which God has canceled the only debt that could ever harm us, put our confidence in Him and live according to His Word? Or will we continue to allow our lives to be driven by and enslaved to our wants, and thus, our debts? Leigh and I made a decision early on in our marriage that has served us well. It was a decision partly guided by my profession and the reality that my earning potential over a lifetime had a very real ceiling. Unless we won the lottery, we were never going to have an abundance of things. Therefore, we made the decision that we would never stretch. We would never buy things we knew we could not afford, and by following that simple rule of thumb, we have no debt today other than the debt on our house which we will pay off in less than eight years. It's hard, because we see what others have. We're human, and we struggle with the "wants" in life, but we chose to resist what we heard others describe. "We got a great deal on a house. It was a little beyond our price range, but we couldn't pass it up" or "That vacation cost us a fortune, but it was worth it." Those decisions at the time may seem wise, but they slowly dig a hole of debt that becomes more and more of a prison with each passing year. Look at your life. Be wise. Don't stretch. Live within your means so that you find freedom in your money and the blessing of living a generous life. Remember, God has revealed His ultimate desire for us which is to live debt-free in the abundance of His grace, love, and provision. If we trust that, then I think we'll start putting in place the necessary practices that will get us out of debt and on the path to generosity and freedom.

CHAPTER 4

READY, SHOOT, AIM

"For those who are according to the flesh set their minds on the things of the flesh, but those who are according to the Spirit, the things of the Spirit." (Romans 8:5)

"Money often costs too much." (Ralph Waldo Emerson)

I think it is safe to say that I am a person who moves fairly quickly through life. I don't let any grass grow under my feet, and sometimes that is a character flaw because it gets me in trouble. For example: While playing church softball at Signal Mountain Presbyterian a few years back, I had a little altercation with the youth pastor from the Baptist church as I rounded third base. We had gone into extra innings, he was their third baseman, and he did something that was clearly in the wrong (at least in my mind!) Of course, I expressed my sentiments about that to him in a fairly direct manner. Rev. Bill Dudley, the pastor I worked for at the time, was a master at knowing how to yank my chain. He had heard about this little altercation, so before the first service that next Sunday, he called me into his office and said that the pastor at the Baptist church had called him to express some concerns about my sportsmanship in the game and requesting a meeting with me later that week. I went nuts. I was fuming. I started grousing about Bill's office, pacing, fuming, and Bill says, "Don't worry. Don't do anything. I'll send an elder with you to meet with him and we'll work it all out." He knew good and well I wasn't going to do that. I chewed on it all through the first service, and then as soon as I got back to my office, I picked up the phone and called the Baptist church and amazingly the pastor answered. So, I said, "Pastor, I want to talk to you about this whole sportsmanship thing at the softball game Friday night. I don't think you really understand what happened, and I am distressed that you had to call my boss about it. I don't appreciate that one bit. If you have a problem with me, you come to me." When I finished my rant, there was a long pause, and then he said, "David, I don't know what you are talking about. I didn't call Bill and I don't know anything about a softball game." Right at that moment, I knew I'd been had. I said sheepishly to the pastor, "You didn't call Bill about the softball game the other night?" "No," he says. "I don't know anything about that." As soon as I hung up the phone, my face quite red, I heard the sound of uproarious laughter in the hall outside my door as my wife, the other pastors, and Bill had all been outside listening to the whole thing, knowing I was going to make a fool of myself. I certainly did not let them down. I didn't think about it. I didn't ask anyone else for advice. I just reacted, a classic example of a behavior pattern known as "Ready. Shoot. Aim."

As embarrassing as that was in my own life, my bet is that I am not the only one who has done something like that. Maybe not all of us, but at least some of us, are occasionally tempted to react to things too quickly. We tend to take action first and ask questions later. My assistant has actually been quite helpful to me in this area as she often gets me to wait for twenty-four hours after writing emails before sending them. I'm sure none of you have ever sent an email that you later regretted. There's this sinful, prideful part of us that instinctively says, "I'm right. I know what's best and I am going to do this right now." The result of that is often ready, shoot, aim. This is especially painful when it involves our money. We can be very impulsive with our money and our spending. I'm sure none of you have ever bought on impulse or made a purchase to make yourself feel better about some disappointment. We are especially prone to a "ready, shoot, aim" decision-making pattern in our finances because we consider that area to be largely private. We don't talk to others about our money. It's none of their business, so we rationalize the situation into our favor. We deserve it. We earned it. We've had a bad week. Whatever. We think we know what's best, so we keep it to ourselves.

Personally, I am a pro at this. I met this guy in Ft. Myers who I didn't know that well, but he sounded smart and showed me all these graphs and pie charts on his computer about his investment research. I didn't ask anyone and I didn't investigate it to any degree. I just gave him $10,000 out of my savings account because I thought I knew best. In just a few short weeks, he had managed to turn it into $4400 and then $2000 and then I got out. It was an $8000 lesson in ready, shoot, aim. Even as I write this now, I am furious with myself over how dumb a decision I made. It was misguided and ill-informed, not so much because I made a bad investment, but because I never sought counsel in the process, not even from my wife.

We do it all the time, and it's this idea that brings us to my text in **Psalm 106** which is a "mini" history lesson on the history of Israel, especially as it relates to the miraculous nature in which God delivered her from Egypt and brought her to the promised land. The Psalmist gives thanks to the Lord and praises the Lord for all that He has done, but he is also very descriptive of Israel's pattern of relating to God. He says in verse 13, *"but they soon forgot what He had done and did not wait for his counsel. In the desert they gave in to their cravings; so He gave them what they asked for."* Here is an entire nation that has been redeemed from slavery. They had watched God part the Red Sea and provide sustenance for them in the desert. They received the hope of a promised land, but none of that was good enough. This Psalm says they quit seeking His counsel and started doing what they wanted. It wasn't just that they didn't listen, they weren't even asking anymore. It was the same in **Judges 21:25** which says, "In those days, Israel had no king; all the people did whatever seemed right in their own eyes." I would think that sounds a bit familiar. It was ready, shoot, aim. They sought no counsel because in their minds, they were king. They did what they wanted when they wanted. God's answer, then, was to give them what they asked for. He said, "Fine. If you are not satisfied with Me and you want something else, if you won't listen to Me or consider My wisdom, then I'll let you have what you want and you'll see how far that gets you." It was the same in Romans 1 when Paul writes, "Although they claimed to be wise, they became fools and exchanged the glory of immortal God for images made to look like mortal man....because of this, God gave them over to shameful lusts." God let them see the consequences of following their own gods. Even though they had just seen God do these great things, they quickly slipped into the same pattern we have discussed. So, from the experience of Israel and the truth of this Psalm, what can we learn?

We All Need Counsel

First, as simple as this sounds, *we all need counsel*, and this is especially true when it comes to our money. Let me share a few of the verses contained in the book of Proverbs that relate to this issue of counsel:

Proverbs 10:8: *"The wise in heart accept counsel, but a chattering fool comes to ruin."*

Proverbs 11:14: *"For lack of guidance a nation falls, but many advisers make victory sure."*

Proverbs 12:15: *"The way of a fool seems right to him, but a wise man listens to advice."*

Proverbs 15:22: *"Plans fail for lack of counsel, but with many advisers they succeed."*

Proverbs 19:20: *"Listen to advice and accept instructions, and in the end you will be wise."*

Proverbs 8:10-11: *"Choose my instruction instead of silver . . . for wisdom is more precious than rubies."*

There are many more, but I think you get my point. God's book of wisdom is filled with His commands for us to seek counsel. Now why do you suppose it is repeated? Why do you think God is emphasizing this? The reason is because He knows us, and He knows our tendency is always going to be a temptation to only listen to ourselves. He is saying, "People, you need counsel. Pay attention. Seek it out. Listen. You need people speaking into your lives." The Bible says we are fools if we don't do this. We need good counsel, but when it comes to our money, we won't do it. We'll get counsel on just about everything else. We will share intimately with others on nearly every other subject: our marriage, our health, our jobs, our children – but when is the last time you ever heard anyone share openly about their money? They'll say, "I got a great deal on a house" but they don't ever tell you the number. They'll say "I got promoted and got a great raise" but they won't tell you how much. It's just not done, and because it's not, we have no accountability to God's Word as to our faithfulness. I'll never forget a few years ago when I asked one of our elders, Scott Lee, to share his testimony in worship regarding his personal generosity. You could have heard a pin drop when he announced to the entire church what his salary was AND how much he gave to the church the preceding year. It was stunning because no one ever does that. One of the most transformational experiences of my life happened when I lived on Signal Mountain and took part in a small men's group. There were only four of us, but that allowed for great depth. We had spent several months talking about money, and then someone had the great idea to bring accountability into the mix. We agreed that meant we were going to have to share our personal financial situation. For the next four weeks, each one of us took a week to lay out our full financial position – what we made, what we gave, what we saved, what we had invested – everything. At that point, as we moved forward, we were then able to give each other true counsel as we thought about the financial decisions we were making and God's call on us to be faithful stewards.

That same principle has now come to life in my current church. Each year, I teach our new members class on generosity. I talk about the Biblical foundations and the church's expectations for faithful stewardship. I then tell them exactly how much I make, what I give, what I save – because I truly believe that I cannot ask people in the church to do what I am not willing to do myself. Plus, I have the accountability of the team in our finance office! They know exactly what I give and what I make, so if I stood and said otherwise, they would know I was a fraud. Why is this important? We'll never get free in our finances and our giving until we start seeking counsel, and you can't get good counsel unless you are honest with people about exactly where you are. I'm not saying you need to tell everyone, but I am saying you need to tell a few. Otherwise, we fall right back into Romans 1. No one else knows, so we do what we want, and if we're not careful, God will allow us to experience exactly where that leads.

This demands a humble, teachable spirit. It takes a humble person to say, "Can you help me with this" because that statement acknowledges your own weakness. Counsel is going to be no good to you if you are too arrogant to pay attention to that counsel. I've had occasions where I'm working with an employee, trying to share some counsel with him, and he has this look on his face like he just wants to roll his eyes. Perhaps you have seen this on your teenager's face. The reality is we all have blind spots. We all have places in our lives that we don't see so well, thus, we need others to help us see them. I used to think my golf swing looked like Jack Nicklaus until someone put it on video. It was then that I realized that my perception of what I was doing was nowhere near the reality. So it is for all of us. We need to always have an open spirit to the advice and counsel of others so that we are always growing, always learning, always yielding to the work of God's Spirit.

So, in light of that, let me ask you: Who do you have who speaks into your life? Who are your counselors, and how are you actively engaging them? If you don't have anyone, then you need to ask yourself why not and consider whether or not you are willing to humble yourself to seek it in the future. When I was fresh out of seminary, one of the things that frustrated me was that my work never got evaluated any more. I used to get a sheet of paper back from my professors with numerous comments and ideas for improvement, but once I got out of seminary and began working, that didn't happen. As a result, I struggled to continue to learn and grow. As I lived in that season, I finally asked four men to evaluate every sermon I gave, every lesson I taught, and to do that in detail. I still have the letters they wrote me. What they said was formative to me. It was not always easy to receive, but it was tremendously helpful. We need counselors, and likely we need more than one. Your counsel may come from a range of people in your life, so let's think for a moment about where we can receive wise counsel if we currently lack it.

Briefly, I think there are three primary places where you and I should be seeking counsel. The first one and most obvious is **the Lord.** Psalm 32:8 says, "*I will instruct you and teach you in the way you should go. I will counsel you and watch over you.*" James 1:5 says, "*If any of you lack wisdom, he should ask God, who gives generously.*" Perhaps you noticed lately that the world is full of experts. All you need is a YouTube channel or an Instagram account that allows you to make videos and pontificate on various subjects. People may have no background or education on anything, and yet they act like experts and many of us get lured in! There are a host of people trying to tell you what to do, and we get sucked into that fairly easily. However, we need to be careful that the counsel we seek first is from the Lord through prayer. As we do that, we should also be listening to His voice by investing time in the Word. God has already said a lot, and often I find Him speaking to me and answering my prayers by what I read in His Word. Howard Dayton shared that there are 2350 verses in the Bible related to money, more than any other single subject. If God has so much to say on this subject, don't you think it would be wise for us to seek that counsel? That's exactly what we're doing in this book.

Once you have sought the Lord and His Word, the second place you should go is to **your spouse**, or in the case of a student or child, **your parents**. When you get married, God takes two people and makes them one, which means that no decision, no experience is ever separate any more. There is always going to be some connection, some impact from one to the other by the Holy Spirit, and we need to pay attention to that. My wife is often the greatest vessel of God's counsel in my life. If God has called you to be married and has a plan for that marriage, then He is not going to be giving each of you conflicting data. You need to listen to one another which implies you are talking about it. Sadly, that is often not the case in many marriages. Leigh and I lead a church marriage retreat every other year, and one of the exercises we have couples do is to sit in chairs back to back and we ask them to write down the answers to the following questions: How much is your monthly household income? How much debt do you carry? How much did you give away last year? What is the current balance on credit cards? Most couples did not both know the answers; overwhelmingly, only one knew the correct data. When God creates a marriage – a husband and wife where two become one – that means everything. It certainly includes your money. Separate bank accounts are at odds with the covenant of marriage. There is no longer "your money and my money." It is all God's money and it is given by him to you as a couple. It's "our" money. Don't get lulled into thinking that you need separate accounts because they will only draw a wedge between you as you lose the accountability to each other. You can easily begin trying to conceal your spending, and that never leads anywhere healthy.

Third, seek the counsel of **others** who you know to be wise and trustworthy: friends, men or women in your small group, people you know or have observed in business, siblings or others who know you well. Bill Dudley, whom I mentioned at the beginning, is one of my most trusted counselors. Rarely do I make a major decision without asking him what he thinks. I don't always do what he says, but I want the input. One of the obstacles we have to overcome is thinking, "Well, I don't want to bother them." Honestly, who would not respond well to someone asking, "Could I spend some time with you for a few minutes to get your advice about something?" By definition, you are affirming and building up that person. Pray about who to ask, and then ask. When it comes to money and finances, we especially need to find people who share our Kingdom perspective who can help us make sound financial decisions and hold us accountable to those decisions.

Then last, beyond those interpersonal relationships, we get counsel from afar by **reading books or journals**. I am counseled regularly by a number of authors whom I have found to be wise and insightful. **Money, Sex and Power** by Richard Foster and **The Treasure Principle** by Randy Alcorn are two classics worth your time. Before I move on, let me also add one thing: There is some counsel we need to be wary of. As I said earlier, there are a lot of people who will line up to be your counselors, and many of them do not have your best interest or God's Kingdom in mind. When God called you, He didn't call you to check your brain at the door. If someone starts to give you advice, you always need to test that and hold it up against God's Word and then seek confirmation of it from other sources. If it's true, it will hold up. If it's false, you will find a lot of conflicting data.

Having said all of that, wouldn't it be great if it were that easy? We would just seek good counsel and everything in our lives would be fine, but we know it doesn't work that way. The reality is, we often refuse counsel or fail to seek it, so we need to figure out why. The answer is found in the roots of our human heart as we see in Genesis 3. When the serpent comes to Eve to get her to eat the fruit, what does she do? Just like Israel after her, God had acted and given her good things—a beautiful place to live, food and shelter, purpose and work, a husband—but she quickly forgets all that when confronted by the serpent. She does not ask God about this new information she has received. She does not consult Adam. As Psalm 106 says, she just gave in to her craving. She was so enthralled at the prospect of being her own god that she was content to listen only to her voice, to her heart, for what she wanted. That's what we all do. That's why we don't seek counsel, especially the Lord's counsel because we know we may not get the answer we want.

Have you ever noticed how some people seek counsel? They want to do something, so they just keep going from person to person until they find someone who validates what they have wanted to do all along. I always smile a bit when someone tells me they are leaving the church "because you don't preach what I want to hear." It happens. We do that with God. We don't like what He says, so we just go find other counselors. Oswald Chambers wrote, "There is no doubt that God has let us know His commandments. It's not that we don't know them, but that we do not do them, and then gradually, as a consequence of such disobedience, we no longer know what is right."

That's what happened to Israel. Not only were they not listening, but they weren't even asking anymore. They just did what they wanted, and eventually, God showed them the consequences of such choices. And doing what we want shows up in three primary ways: discontent, pride, and impatience. Without doubt, discontent drives your choices and decisions, especially as they relate to money. That is why our economy finds itself in the place it's in. A consumerist culture by definition must constantly create discontent in the mind of the consumer to stimulate more spending. We always want more. Instead of finding contentment in what God has provided, we want more, so we ignore whatever it is He might be saying to us about our resources.

Then our pride tells us that we don't need counsel. Instead, we help ourselves! Isn't it amazing the number of self-help programs and books and DVD's that are on the market today? You can help yourself succeed, have better self-esteem, cook better, weigh less, earn more, think smarter, feel softer—you name it and it's there. Even so, when we try to help ourselves find meaning or peace or significance, it doesn't work, at least not in the long term. University of Minnesota research indicates that 80% of people who make changes on January 1 fall back to prior patterns by February 14. Dr. Edward Miller, Dean of the Medical Faculty at Johns Hopkins, said that 70% of coronary bypass patients revert to unhealthy habits within two years of the operation. You don't have to be a research specialist to know that when it comes to helping ourselves, we don't do such a great job. We need the help and counsel of others.

Then our impatience gets us. Verse 13 says they *"did not wait for his counsel."* The implication is that God had something to say, but they were not willing to wait for it. John Calvin writes, "The insatiable nature of our desires is astonishing in that scarcely a single day is allowed to God to gratify them. For should He not immediately satisfy them, we at once become impatient, and are in danger of falling into despair." (**John Calvin's Bible Commentary on the Psalms 93-119**) God wants to advise you, but if you don't wait for that advice, then how are you ever going to walk in His will? If you are always acting with impatience, you are going to ruin the plan. When I was little, I always used to snoop around looking for where my parents had hidden my Christmas presents, and often, I found them. However, what I learned was that my impatience robbed me of what my sisters experienced on Christmas morning. The whole plan got messed up because I was not willing to wait. We want desperately to operate on our time, but if we will wait for God to speak, He will, and our lives will be richer and better for it.

The raw truth is that we need counsel because this life is flat hard. Being faithful is not easy. Being wise stewards is not easy. Os Guiness writes, "In an age when comfort and convenience are unspoken articles of our modern bill of rights, the Christian faith is not a license to entitlement, a prescription for an easy-going spirituality, or a how-to manual for self-improvement. The cross of Jesus Christ runs crosswise to all our human ways of thinking." (**Prophetic Untimeliness: A Challenge to the Idol of Relevance**, page 67) The cross runs counter to all our human ways of thinking, so if it does, then it stands to reason that we need the counsel of others to help us think as God would have us—not born out of our sinful hearts—but rather living faithfully as His sons and daughters. You are His redeemed and beloved child, but recognize, today, you also need counsel to continue to live out the life He has called you to; not "ready, shoot, aim," but faithfully using all of His resources and gifts in ways that honor and glorify Him. May we humble ourselves and pursue that this day and in the days to come.

CHAPTER 5

A DYING BREED

"The integrity of the upright guides them, but the unfaithful are destroyed by their duplicity." (Proverbs 11:3)

"All believers must guard the heart and the mind and strive to walk before Christ and with each other in integrity." (David Alley, *20 Things to Know About Apostles Today*)

Without question, money can often bring out the worst in people, including myself. Families will often get along perfectly well until someone dies and an inheritance is involved. Suddenly, people who have gotten along well for decades are in crisis, and it's all because of money. As I was preparing for this message, I stumbled upon a website that had a "Financial Honesty Quiz" that helps you gauge the level of your dishonesty in regard to your money. For example, one question read: **Have you ever led your significant other to believe there is more or less in your "mad money" stash than there really is?** Perhaps your answer would be no- or maybe s/he has only a *slight* misrepresentation - or perhaps it depends on what your definition of 'is' is.

Another sample question: **You're splurging at a high end steakhouse ordering the 20-ounce bone-in ribeye with crab meat and béarnaise; the wine flows like water and you cap if off with slices of orange cake all around. You figure this is going to cost you a fortune, only it's not quite as bad because your waitress forgot to put your ribeye on your check. Do you tell her?** Perhaps your answer would be "of course I would" – or maybe it's "no, but I would leave her a really, really nice tip"; or maybe it's "no way because it's not my fault."

Last question: **You take your 12-year-old daughter and her pals to Disney. You could save a bundle *if* you tell the cashier that they are all UNDER 12, not ACTUALLY 12, which would be totally and unequivocally believable. Do you?** Sure. Who wouldn't? It's win-win. The park still makes out, and you save a few bucks. Or, absolutely not. Or you'd be tempted, if it didn't involve a child who would doubtless overhear: bad example, and all that.

I could keep going, but I think you get the idea. At the end of the test, they score your answers and give you a little report back. I decided to take the test and in the interest of full disclosure, my summary report begins with, "You're sometimes tempted to get tricky with the truth, or at least a bit vague." Ouch! Is it just me, or does money tempt us to make choices that push the boundaries of honesty and integrity?

Further, if we don't learn that lesson, then we are destined to lead a life that makes constant rationalizations for unethical decisions because in our mind, the end justifies the means. The world was shocked, but I dare say not completely surprised, when Bernie Madoff admitted to a $50 billion scam. Congressional committees drilled President Obama's choice for Treasury Secretary, Timothy Geithner, when they discovered that he had not paid $36,000 in self-employment tax that he owed. They poked and prodded because they needed to know: Did he intentionally do this, or was it an "honest" mistake? I was talking to someone in the financial management business who said the financial dishonesty of others has now made it more expensive for him in that he has to go to greater lengths to ensure his clients that his business is, in fact, honest and that such dishonesty would never happen.

One of the "reality" shows on FOX television a few years back was a production called "Lie to Me" in which the advertisements say, "Every person lies three times every ten minutes. We know how to spot them." We see the dishonesty and we are troubled by it, but our little quiz raises the question for us: How honest are we? Are we consistent in following our own moral and ethical code of conduct? Does our spending, our use of money, reflect the theological foundations on which we have built our lives, or do we compartmentalize our finances as if they, somehow, fall into a different category that has a different set of rules? Are we living with integrity in our stewardship before the Lord?

Those are the questions that bring us again to *1 Chronicles 29*. David is concluding his time as King over Israel. His son Solomon is about to succeed him, but before that happens, God has charged them with the great task of building a temple for the Lord, a dwelling place where the Lord would come down and in which the people could worship. As such, the temple would be a means of extending God's Kingdom in the world. It becomes necessary then for David to call God's people to give to the Lord with wholehearted devotion, but he also calls them to bring that offering with a particular quality: honesty of heart.

In **verse 16**, David affirms, yet again, that God is the owner of all things. He says all of our abundance comes from the Lord; it belongs to Him. Then, in **verse 17**, David brings what may be one of the most challenging verses in all of Scripture: *"I know my God that you test the heart and are pleased with integrity. All these things have I given willingly and with honest intent."* As we look at these specific words, what does God have to teach us, today, in relationship to personal and financial integrity?

What God Expects

First, in our relationship with God, His expectation of

us is that *we will live our lives with integrity*, an integrity based on our obedience to His Word. David is absolutely clear in his declaration that our **integrity pleases God**. If God is pleased by our integrity of life and heart, then we know that such is His desire for us. It is His expectation. Paul said in ***Philippians 2:12***, *"Therefore, my dear friends, as you have always obeyed not only in my presence, but also in my absence — continue to work out your salvation."* Paul reinforces 1 Chronicles 29:17. God is essentially saying, "I expect you to live the same when I'm gone as when I'm here. I expect you to live with integrity." God expects us to live our lives in ways that honor Him, whether we are in the presence of other believers or not, whether we are in the presence of our spouse or not, whether we are in the presence of our boss or not. No matter who we are with, our behavior should match the faith we profess.

I've shared with you before how funny it can be when I play golf with strangers. You show up to play at a course as a twosome and you get paired with two other guys. The round begins, and invariably, someone hits a bad shot. They stomp around and cuss and swear. Then later, one of them will ask me, "So, what do you do?" "Well, I pastor a church." Suddenly, they get this look of terror on their face, become very apologetic, and stop swearing for the rest of the round. Whenever that happens, I want to say, "Why change your behavior now? You are obviously aware of a standard that calls you to a better use of your language. That standard has been set by God, not me. Do you not think God is aware of what you're doing when I'm not here?" Do you see what we do? We live our lives sometimes as if God is not present, as if God, somehow, cannot see us or is not aware of our actions. *"Not only in my presence, but also in my absence."* That's called integrity. Ask yourself that question today: do you live the same way when people are watching as you do when you're alone?   And do you live under the illusion that God has off hours and is unaware of some of your actions? No, none of us are perfect. We will surely miss the mark, but integrity of heart and life is one of the greatest things we possess. We should be guarding it more carefully.

Further, our integrity before the Lord is based on our love for Him. Remember, David was "a man after God's own heart." He loved the Lord, and as such, he was willing to make a huge gift to the Lord with the utmost honesty. However, as Howard Dayton points out, you cannot love someone AND be dishonest. Ask any spouse who has endured the pain of betrayal. You are not loving someone when you are being dishonest with them, so dishonesty and love are incongruous. You cannot do both at the same time. You either love them and live before them with integrity, or you betray that love and live before them dishonestly. The former is the foundation for healthy relationship, and the latter is the ground for destruction. Not only is this true in our relationship with God, but in every relationship we have. You can't love and be dishonest at the same time.

This naturally begs the question of our secret lives, those parts of our lives that we think no one knows about. I mentioned in an earlier chapter how some couples will get separate bank accounts. Those often become the foundation for secrecy, for habits and behaviors that we keep from others. Many of us live one way in the world, one way in front of our friends, one way with our family, and one way when we're alone. Unfortunately, when we are alone, we can easily lean towards darkness. We rationalize that we "deserve" to do what we want because no one else understands the burdens we carry, or our spouse is not giving us enough attention, or God didn't come through in the way we thought He should, so we decide to punish Him by our blatant disobedience. When we are disciples of Jesus Christ, we are His disciple all the time. It's 24/7. The closer our behaviors align with God's Word and will, the more integrity we possess, and the more consistent our behaviors will be. When "who you are" is consistent, your integrity of life is growing. So, sometimes we need to ask ourselves the hard question: Do you secretly channel money into separate accounts for later use? Does your greed force your spending to such levels that your external life is nothing more than a facade? Or is it a secret life of pornography? Is it a secret attraction to or relationship with a person other than your spouse? Is it an angry and abusive personality? Is it an addiction? Where is your secret life and how is God speaking to you to begin to change such that you may please Him by your integrity?

Our Integrity is a Significant Part of Our Witness

Second, *our integrity is a significant part of our witness*. Think about why David was concerned about his integrity. He knew it would help influence the people of Israel, one way or the other. If he demonstrated financial integrity, then many would follow him, but if he failed in it, then very few would follow. As I said in an earlier chapter, if I wasn't honest about my own giving, the finance department in our church would instantly know I was a fraud. No one would follow. It's good accountability for me, but that integrity should be there regardless. In a recent survey of 20 year olds who grew up in the church but who no longer attend, one of the primary reasons they listed for not attending was the hypocrisy of church leaders. I know that no one is going to be perfect, but that group was making a significant statement about integrity. They were saying it was currently lacking in the lives of those in leadership, and its absence hurt the witness and effectiveness of the church. If I spoke on stewardship, but it was revealed that I gave nothing to the church, how would that affect you? If I spoke on marriage, but it was revealed that I was out at strip clubs in the evening, how would that affect you? I think you get the point.

I had breakfast with someone who had been visiting our church, and he said he wanted to get to know me because sometimes the guy in the pulpit was not the same guy in reality. I thought, "What a terribly sad statement and such an indictment on Christian leaders today." Integrity in our faith is the foundation of our Christian witness. If we claim the name of Christ, we should live with integrity and that integrity is attractive to the world by its uniqueness. Understand, God knows our hearts. David says in verse 17 that he "tests" our hearts. It's not like He doesn't know. It's time to quit pretending. Let's own up to who and what we are, and let's endeavor to please God by the integrity of our lives.

God Expects Integrity in Our Finances

Third, *God expects integrity in our finances*. Money is no different than any other area of life, yet if there is one area that we tend to compartmentalize as separate from God, it's our money. We'll work to live with integrity in every other area, but we rationalize that there's a different set of rules when it comes to our money. God, through David, says "No." He says in verse 17, *"All these things I have given willingly and with honest intent."*

In other words, "Lord, I am giving this to you with integrity. My heart is honest and sincere before you." As sure as I say that, I would imagine you would find that hard to refute. It's right there in the Bible. However, many of you are thinking, "Well, yes, but I don't feel that. I don't feel a desire to let go of my finances. I don't feel particularly generous. In fact, I feel the opposite. I feel insecure because I don't think I have enough. I have no idea what my future holds with my job or my income; bills are piling up. I'm stuck. I also feel inferior because I don't have as much as some others around me. I feel like it is mine because I have worked so hard to obtain it." All those thoughts are basic human realities. That's fair. That's where many people are. So, if that's the case, and we love the Lord, how do we find freedom in our money such that we begin to live with integrity in our finances and our giving?

The answer is found in our relationship with God. Here's the key: If we want to live with financial integrity, we must realize that integrity is grounded in our honest and sincere relationship with the Lord. Look at David. His primary concern was his relationship with God such that his financial decisions were made in consultation with God. David was called to serve the Lord. He was called to build this temple. He goes to the Lord. He worships. He leads the people in worship. Without question, I think one of the things that keep us honest is a healthy respect and reverence for the One who sits on the throne. If we never worship, it is easy to lose our sense of reverence and awe for God, and our obedience suffers in the process. David prays. In that prayer, he acknowledges God's nature. He understands the glory and majesty of the true owner, and as a result, he makes his gift to the Lord. What a novel idea: consulting God in our finances!

While that makes perfect sense, we still don't do it. Maybe you recall an old advertising campaign for a financial services company that said, "When E. F. Hutton talks, people listen." I had no idea at the time who E.F. Hutton was, but if everyone was listening, I figured I'd better find out. Similarly, God's been talking about money for thousands of years, but unlike E.F. Hutton, we're NOT listening to Him. We never consult Him. We never ask. We just act and react according to our wants or needs. Remember, we NEED counsel. Like David, we need to go to the Lord and ask, "How, O God, would you have me spend this money which You have provided? You are the Lord. There is no one like You. You are the owner of these things, not me. I want to have integrity before You as I spend it, so what would You have me do?" Perhaps it's time to add such a prayer to our time with God.

Instead of doing that, we go to our financial accounts, we look at our bills, we look at our debt, and we say, "Well, based on what I have left over, we'll give this." Like it or not, that kind of decision lacks financial integrity. It's a violation of your walk with God. It's a violation because you did not consult Him on the decisions you made to spend your money in the first place, decisions which now lead you to believe there is nothing left to give. It's the opposite of what God wants. God calls us to bring in the first fruits of the harvest. Our first check is to the Lord as a sign of our reverence for Him and our trust in His provision. We never give God out of the leftovers. He calls us to *tithe* to the church as the vessel of His Kingdom work, His divinely created bride through whom He is revealing Himself to the world. He then calls us to make offerings, gifts beyond the tithe that support the widow, the orphan and the alien – the needs of the less fortunate, Christian and non-Christian alike. However, because we have not consulted the Lord on these things, we now find ourselves living beyond our means, not giving with integrity, and thus the church struggles to do what God has called her to do.

Allow me to give you an example from First Presbyterian Church: If we assumed that all the members of FPCO made the **average social security retirement income** and tithed on that income, our budget would go up by $3.5 million dollars. It's a staggering number. If just the Christians in this country tithed, it would be enough to feed the entire world for a year. The consequences of our disobedience are painful. Our lack of integrity in our generosity is what keeps the ministry of the church from being extended in the manner God desires. We could do so much more.

I know this is hard. This is the place where the rubber meets the road in our faith. Some of you want to walk out. Some of you wish I would finish or not bring it up altogether. However, let's remember the purpose of the Gospel is to comfort the afflicted and afflict the comfortable. We need to hear the hard things at times so the Spirit can bring conviction. If we find we have not been honest in our lives, whether in our finances or in some other personal dimension, we CAN make it right. God is a gracious and compassionate God who is always willing to welcome us home. Look at your lives honestly – repent – and seek the Lord's strength for your obedience in the future.

The way to get rid of that uncomfortable feeling is to do what you know you need to do to make it right. Confess the dishonesty to the Lord and then to that person, and restore whatever has been gained or taken dishonestly. It's something that doesn't roll off our tongues very easily, but you may want to try it. "Honey, I was not honest with you about where I was the other night. I have not been honest with you about what I've been doing on the computer." "Lord, I have not been honest with you about how I use what belongs to you." Then, just as David did, set a course for personal obedience. There are often consequences for our dishonesty and you may have to live in the midst of those for a time, but the end result, like David, will be the joy of building a life and a witness, a temple, if you will, where the Lord can come to dwell. Now is the time to do that.

Sometimes, that process can be very complex. I have often spoken to people living in the web of their own deceit. The dishonesty becomes so large they can't remember all the places where it must be unwound. Have you ever gotten into a place like that? You tell one lie and then you have to tell a series of others to cover the first one, and then it just snowballs? The larger that web becomes the more pressure you live under to keep the web from getting torn down. It's a house of cards, and I have never failed to find that when those cards come crashing down around people, while difficult, the overriding feeling they experience is one of relief. They are finally free from having to keep up the facade.

Friends, God wants you to know freedom from the traps of your own deceit, the freedom that comes from living a life that is honest, one marked by integrity in all things so you never have to worry or fear what you have told one person or what statement may one day catch up to you. We may work hard to keep up the façade, but deep down inside, you want that relief. You want that peace. I pray that you will take the steps necessary in whatever area of your life you may need to, but especially as it relates to your money, so that you are living with integrity and honest intent before the Lord. What you'll find when you live this way is that you will be a faithful witness to the world in a way that is radically different, and you'll find the presence and peace of God alive in you in ways you have never known before. As God has called us, may we live with integrity in all things, not only in the presence of others, but much more so in their absence.

CHAPTER 6

THE PARADOX OF GIVING

"She, out of her poverty, put in everything." (Mark 12:44)

"He is no fool who gives what he cannot keep to gain what he cannot lose." (Jim Elliott)

I want to begin this chapter by sharing a few letters with you: C, D, B, C. While you may be thinking that is an acronym for the Crazy Drinking Beer Club, those are actually my high school math grades: Algebra 1 and 2, Geometry, and Trigonometry. I hated them and they hated me. I am just one of those people who could never make the numbers add up. I could never make it work, but people who love math love it for that reason: they can always make the numbers work. They can always find the answer. There's some sort of odd security about it for them.

Math is a very precise, defined science where if you do it right, you get the answer. The same is true in life. We all work very hard to make the numbers work. We're all a bit stressed in the recession these days because it's tougher to make the numbers work, but we make the numbers work for buying a home, for sending our kids to college, for retirement, for vacations, even in family planning. We always need the numbers to work. It makes us feel secure, but let's face it: even when the numbers don't add up, we tend to do what we want anyway.

Let me share a riddle with you. I promise it has no answer.

Three guys walk into a hotel to get a room they are going to share. The clerk charges them $300, so they each plunk down a $100 bill and go upstairs with the bellman. When the bellman comes back, the clerk says he made a mistake and that the room was only $270, so he gives the bellman a $50 bill and says go work it out. Well, the bellman knows they can't split a $50, so he exchanges it for five ten dollar bills. He decides to pocket two of them for a tip knowing the men would never be the wiser, and then he gives one ten dollar bill to each of the three men. However, here's the problem: It sounds fine, but the numbers don't work. Each man put in $100, but with the returned $10, how much have they paid? $90. 90 x 3 is 270. The bellman has $20 which adds up to $290. Where's the other 10? It all seems logical. It ought to work. The money is all there, but in this case, the numbers don't add up. (Yes, it's all in the telling. Don't stress about the solution. Keep reading!)

Sometimes the numbers don't work, and when they don't, we get anxious. Bothered. Troubled. We don't do well when the numbers don't work. Right now, you are scratching your heads. It makes us feel insecure or unsure. We are reluctant to move or act if we don't feel the numbers work, and that has everything to do with God's call upon our lives to give and the reason we often don't. We just can't make the numbers work.

It is that idea that brings us to our text in **Acts 20:32-38**. It is Paul's farewell speech to the Ephesian elders at Miletus. They are parting, and most likely, will never see each other again, so you can imagine the poignancy of the moment. It is very emotional. They weep. They embrace. They kiss. It is a rare scene, indeed. However, what I want you to notice is that in this final discourse, this moment when he is sharing the very last words he will ever speak with these leaders, he recalls the words of Jesus, "*It is more blessed to give than to receive.*" He says, "My example among you was that I did not covet what you had; I did not take from you, but instead I gave." Why does Paul say that in such a moment? Why does Paul go there? Think about it. If you were parting with a group of your friends just prior to your death, would you be inclined to share your thoughts with them on generosity? I highly doubt it. It makes no sense to us, and yet Paul takes up that subject with the Ephesian elders. Clearly, he says it because he knows it is one of the most critical things Jesus said, and in the Economy of God, that's how the numbers work. It is more blessed to give than to receive. The word here for "blessed" is a word commonly used in Scripture that means "blessed or happy." In other words, you are going to feel better. You are going to be more content with what you have because you see it as a means of God's provision. You are going to experience more contentment and satisfaction when you give than when you receive because your heart is becoming more aligned with the heart of God.

Even so, I have no doubt people balked at that then just as surely as they balk at that today. It makes no sense. Why? It makes no sense because the numbers don't work within the parameters of this world's economy. It runs contrary to how our current system operates. Let me turn into "math teacher" mode. I have always dreamed of teaching math, and this is actually a math that makes sense to me. It's God's math. Normally, in our world, $1 - 1 = 0$. If you have something and you give it away, you are left with nothing. $1 - 1 = 0$. However, in the Economy of God, it does not work that way. In God's economy, Jesus says $1 - 1 = >1$. If we have something and we give it away, the result is NOT that we are left with nothing, but we will always have more than we had to begin with. We are blessed more by giving than receiving. It's God's new math, and I love it. God reminds us of this constantly in Scripture.

Psalm 112:5: *"Good will come to him who is generous and lends freely, who conducts his affairs with justice."*

Proverbs 19:17: *"He who is kind to the poor lends to the Lord, and he will reward him for what He has done."*

Luke 6:35: *"Love your enemies, do good to them, and lend to them without expecting to get anything back. THEN your reward will be great."*

It's not hard to grasp. You do what God says. You give away what He has given to you in a faithful manner, and you get back more than you gave. Now before you start assuming something I do not mean, let me be very clear: this does that mean you are going to get back more money. You might, but that is not what the promise means. However, you will get back MORE. Remember what I said in the very first chapter: the Economy of God forces you to define true wealth. When you live in this economy, you are going to receive things of far greater value than anything you could experience in this earthly realm. You receive back more than you gave, but those things are going to be far beyond monetary things. They will be things like joy and peace. They will be things like the satisfaction that comes when seeing the hand of God at work through your life.

As good as that may sound, we are still not doing it, and we are not doing it because we have a problem. I'm not sure we actually believe it. We can't launch out and live into this because in the back of our heads the numbers still don't work. We are stuck at 1 - 1 = 0. How do we move forward? If this is where we are and we see the possibility, but we can't get around the numbers, then what do we do?

Have the Courage to Attempt It

First, to live into this new Economy, you have to *have the courage to attempt it*. It is one of those things that is hard to believe until you experience it. I have shared with you before the old axiom that goes, "Progress, without the benefit of prior experience is, for the most part, unbelievable." If I went over to the interior of Africa and found a young man who had never ventured outside his village and then showed him an airplane and said, "That huge thing is going to fly in the sky like a bird," he would never believe me. Why? He has no experience that would point in that direction. He has no frame of reference, and when it comes to our economic understandings, neither do we. We have never actually given God's economy a shot, so we dismiss it. We can't imagine it working as I have just described, so we pan it. We can't make the numbers work, so we dismiss it.

I remember the first time I tried guacamole. Being from Texas, you are raised on good Mexican food, and for years, I resisted the disgusting green, lumpy substance and often my Dad would say, "You don't know what you're missing." He was so right!! When I finally tried it, wow! I can't believe I missed all those years I could have been eating guacamole. There's just nothing better, but I had missed out on it for so long because I was never willing to try it. Let me challenge you: TRY GOD'S ECONOMY. Put out a fleece. Tell the Lord, "I'm going to start living this way and managing my money according to Your numbers." Do it for a year, and if you don't find that you are receiving more than you are giving, quit. Seriously. Quit, but I'd be willing to bet you a lot of money that you won't. I have made this challenge to my church before, and while it has not been taken up by as many people as I would hope, those who have done it have returned to me with amazing stories. Always. Every time. I promise you it works, but you have to have the courage to do it.

Faithful Use of God's Resources Leads to Greater Intimacy With Him

Second, let me reassure you the numbers in the Economy of God work: 1 - 1= >1 because *our faithful use of God's resources leads naturally to greater intimacy with Him*. I know this may sound counter-intuitive, but I often come across people who talk about feeling "distant" from God or that their walk with the Lord has stalled in some way. When I do, a question I always ask is, "How is your giving?" You will find that when you invest your God-given resources in alignment with His will - when you ask the owner and do what He says - you start experiencing a oneness with God that is unique. That should make a lot of sense to us. If you took on a business partner and the two of you invested in something together and built a great building or started some successful business, the two of you would be bound over that success. You'd be closer.

The same is true in our faith. When you partner with God in Kingdom things, there is an intimacy and a sweetness about it that deepens your faith and inspires your growth. As we look at Paul in our text, what created the intimacy with God and with the Body that was expressed in the tears and weeping and emotion of his departure? That intimacy was created by the manner of his life among them. He gave. He sacrificed. He took nothing. He was about what God was about and that giving created intimacy. He got back more than he gave. For Paul, in that moment, you can see that the numbers worked.

Jesus said in **Matthew 6:20-21**, *"Store up for yourselves treasures in heaven, where moth and rust do not destroy and where thieves do not break in and steal, for where your treasure is there will your heart be also."* When you put your treasure in Kingdom places, the world can't take it away, which is why the numbers work. You will never lose on that investment, but that's where people are losing their minds right now in light of the stock market's precipitous decline. Wouldn't it be great to make an investment that was guaranteed to NEVER lose money? As it so happened, Leigh and I received an inheritance following her father's passing that we hoped would put our children through college if we invested it well. We hired a broker, put it in the market, the recession hit, and it has not been worth as much since the day we put it in. After a year, I told our broker, "I can't afford to lose any more money. You have to put that in something that will NOT go down." That's always our fear. We fear we're going to lose money by giving, but that is actually never the case. By giving, you are putting your heart closer to the Lord. Your treasure is in Heaven, so your investment is secure. That's your focus, and that's God's dwelling place. It cannot help but create deeper intimacy and a more meaningful faith in God.

You Develop Christ-like Character

Third, the numbers work in the Economy of God because *when you live accordingly, you develop Christ-like character*. God has said to us that His desire for us is that we become more and more like Christ. Paul writes in **Romans 8:29**, *"For those God foreknew he also predestined to be conformed to the likeness of his Son."* Why did God choose us? He chose us to be like Christ in order that we might reflect who He is to the world. So, what was Christ like? He was one who demonstrated a life of constant love, humility, self-giving and self-sacrifice. Those would be just some of the characteristics that God desires for us to reflect to the world, so that begs the question: how do we become like Christ? Clearly, there are many ways that the Holy Spirit can do that. Prayer and Scripture. Worship. Deep community. Those are all good things, but I am not sure there is a better means of Christ-like character development than when we give. When we give – especially sacrificially, - we will grow in living as Christ: lovingly, sacrificially, selflessly, and humbly. How could we not? Giving puts the Kingdom of God ahead of our kingdom. It puts the needs of others ahead of our needs. It puts our selfish desires in the back seat. If becoming like Christ is the great desire of our God—the reason for which He put us on this planet—then that character development is more significant, more valuable than any monetary thing we might gain for ourselves by living otherwise. Such choices do not make sense according to the numbers of the world, but the numbers work in the Economy of God.

So, if we are at least curious enough at this point to start thinking that maybe the numbers DO work in the Economy of God, then what does that look like? What am I to give and who am I to give it to? This gets us into all the really fun questions. Right now, some of you are thinking, "Oh, gosh, here we go. The pastor is going to reach for my wallet." Not true. I'm not reaching for anything. I'm trying to help you understand a new way of thinking that will actually free you up, but what you do is absolutely up to you. This is about what I want for you, not from you. However, before I do that, I have learned where the human mind tends to go in these conversations. Let's be honest: when it comes right down to it, what you really want to know is exactly how much you owe in order to remain in God's good graces. I mean, if God is in charge and He's telling us to give, then you want me to tell you how much. You want me to tell you the minimum needed to give in order to keep you in the Kingdom. I get it. Welcome to the human race, but the answer is not that easy.

Martin Luther once said that every believer goes through three stages of conversion. The first two are generally interchangeable. It's either your heart and then your head or your head and then your heart. You may have come to faith first because you were so touched and overwhelmed by the love of God. You felt His embrace and the wonder of grace, so you said yes to Him. After that, you began to study God's Word so that you had the theological underpinnings for what you already believed to be true. The reverse can also happen. Those who approach life more intellectually will look at the evidence. They will examine the resurrection accounts, the historicity of Scripture, the growth of the early Church and then decide that yes, Jesus is Lord and Savior of all. It's only later when the love of God touches their hearts in a unique way. We feel in our heart the love of God and we respond. So, our conversation could go either way depending on our personality. Head/heart or heart/head.

However, the third stage of our conversation is always the third part. It is always the last part of the process, and that is the conversion of our will – and that has everything to do with our wallet. In other words, the last part of our conversion is allowing what we know in our head and our heart to actually change the self-centered will of our soul such that we begin to submit to the Lord in personal obedience. We mature to the point where we begin to ask more and more, "What is your will, God?" instead of always wanting our will first. Spiritual maturity is when we want what God wants; it's when our hearts are more closely aligned to His. Therefore, when God commands us to give, we may not understand all the dynamics, but we submit our will (what we want to do with our money) to the will of the Father (what He wants us to do with our money.) That growth leads us to be the generous, caring people that God desires for us to be. I don't think any of us would stand here and say that in the Christian faith, we are called to give nothing. I think we all have an expectation that we will give something, but how much? That's where we have to start exploring how the numbers really work in the Economy of God.

Where Should We Give and How Much?

Well, let's think about that. First, **the offering we make is a sign of our faith in God as THE God among many gods and flows from a heart of worship**. Moses says in **Deuteronomy 12:4**, *"You must not worship the Lord your God in their way . . . seek the place God will choose and there bring your offerings."* I realize that we do not function in the same way that they did in the time of Moses. There are not pagan rituals and festivals on every hill, or are there? If you think about it, we offer ourselves to many gods in this culture without necessarily bowing down to a shrine, but we do it nonetheless. What Moses is saying is, "Who really is your God? Who is primary?" A mature faith is going to recognize that if God is, indeed, the Lord, then that should occupy the priority of one's giving. If God is the Lord, and because of Jesus' work on the cross, He is the singular hope of the world, then there is nothing more important for me or my world than to support that cause. Further, the privilege of doing that is an act of worship. We don't take up an offering during worship because we need to pay the light bill. We take it up as part of leading you to worship God. It's your opportunity to honor the Lord with your personal expression of gratitude and commitment to building

His Kingdom.

Second, **we are not to give as we see fit.** We give as God commands. Ouch! This is where this text gets tough. I'd rather this weren't in here. Moses says in **Deuteronomy 12:8**, *"You are not to do as we do here today, everyone as he sees fit . . . no, you are to bring everything I command you."* So, what does God command we give? Obviously, we think the answer to that is ten percent. We think we are to bring a tithe to the Lord if we are really being obedient. Even then, we get confused about what a tithe actually is. We falsely assume "tithing" means the same thing as "giving something." I hear people say, "I tithe to the church and also FCA and Young Life." What they mean is they gave something, but they do not mean the biblical concept of the tithe. Let's look at the text further.

In **Leviticus 27:30**, we are called to bring what is called The Lord's Tithe to support the priests and the ministry of the tabernacle. This is the gift that supports the ministry of the church and what God wants to do through that institution. This agrees with **Malachi 3** which calls us to *"bring the whole tithe into the storehouse."* The storehouse is the earthly vessel of God's Kingdom—the Church. The Church then finds its expression in particular local churches around the world. Those "storehouses" need the gifts of God's people in order to function and fulfill the call of God. So, that's pretty clear, but then it goes on to say in **Deuteronomy 12:11** to *"bring everything I command you - your burnt offerings and sacrifices, your tithes and special gifts."* Don't look now, but there is MORE to our generosity than just our tithe to the church. We also make an offering on top of that. When you add up all the offerings in this text which the Israelites were called to make, the people were giving away 23% of what they made. Please hear me: I am not suggesting we now become legalistic about this. I am not saying 23% is the number. The New Testament takes the concepts of generosity, bathes them in the grace of God, and makes them about the whole of life. In Christ, we are called to give all of ourselves to the Lord, including our finances. It's total submission, but it's also something we grow in. As you read this book and consider whether the numbers work, just take a step. You may be giving the national average of 2.5% now, so make it 3.5% for the coming year and then try to keep growing until you reach a full ten. At that point, you can start looking at the offerings you want to make and grow accordingly.

This is how Leigh and I have worked it out in our family. We have grown to giving 11% of what we make to the church. On top of that, we support three missionaries and several para-church organizations that total another $200 a month. Then, we make special offerings. For instance, we had a friend in New England trying to adopt a baby from Ethiopia and she needed to raise $30,000 for that, so we gave her $1000. Like many of you, we made a pledge to the Immeasurably More Campaign for $20,000 which we will complete this year. Our offerings were an additional 4% of our total income, so our giving for last year was at 15%. The call of God is for us to give our tithes to the church and offerings to the other things we would like to support, and there are many good causes. Keep in mind, too, the church becomes the primary place because the church receives no other income outside of what you give her. That's it. So God says, first, bring your tithe, then make your offerings. (I also get asked about whether we give on pre-tax or after-tax income. My answer has been do you want to be blessed on the net or the gross?)

Let me also clear up another misconception. We often rationalize that since we give a lot of our time, we don't have to give any money. That is a wonderful human rationalization for compartmentalizing your finances away from the Lord. God calls us to give both. The Lord did not say anywhere in Scripture "Because he gave so much of his time, I asked that he give no money." It's not in there. God calls us to use our gifts to serve. That's our time. We use the abilities we have to serve the Lord. However, He also said, "You need to worship me by giving me a portion of your money which I have given to you." Obviously, we move through some seasons where we are capable of giving more than other seasons. God understands the circumstances of our lives, but even when we are financially struggling, we can still give *something* as an expression of our gratitude and our trust in God's ultimate provision. If we all decided that it was acceptable to give time instead of money, the church would cease to exist. We couldn't function because we would have no resources to do the ministry God has called us to do. It's not one or the other; it's both. We are called to give our time and our money in the Economy of God.

One of my favorite stories is from Brennan Manning, in his book *The Signature of Jesus*. He tells of a group of businessmen who were running late to catch their train after a meeting in New York. They wanted to get home to their families, and in their rush to get to the terminal, one of the men kicked over a slender table on which rested a basket of apples. A ten-year-old boy had been standing there selling apples to pay for his school books and clothes. The five made it to their train, but the one who had hit the table felt a twinge of compassion and guilt over the boy whose table he had turned over. With that, he told his friends to call his wife and tell her that he would be late (clearly in the days before cell phones). He got off the train and when he made it back to the spot, there was the boy, on hands and knees, feeling around for all the apples that had been spilled. The boy was blind. The man began to help the boy collect the apples and in doing so, noticed that some were now split or bruised. Reaching into his pocket, he pulled out a twenty dollar bill and said to the boy, "Here's twenty dollars for the apples I damaged. I hope I didn't ruin your day. God bless you." As the salesman turned to get the next train, the blind boy called after him, saying, "Hey Mister, are you Jesus?"

The reality is, in the Kingdom of God, we are. The grace of Jesus has been given to us, and when we get the grander vision of that blessing, we have the privilege of being Jesus, incarnate, to others, to lift up His church, to take care of His kids, to reach out to the orphan and the widow and the alien. As God in Christ has freely given to us, we become the earthly expression of that sacrificial gift. As people see the witness you are bearing by your generosity, the numbers won't work for them. It will not make sense. Some may even ask you why in the world you give the way you do, but in the Economy of God, the numbers always work. It's a different kind of math. It's more blessed to give than to receive, and I hope you will grow to understand and live into that paradox more and more.

CHAPTER 7

WHAT ABOUT THAT RAINY DAY?

"The plans of the diligent lead surely to abundance, but everyone who is hasty comes only to poverty." (Proverbs 21:5)

"The habit of saving is itself an education; it fosters every virtue, teaches self-denial, cultivates the sense of order, trains to forethought, and so broadens the mind." (Thomas T. Munger)

The older I get, the more observant I have become, and I have noticed something lately: We get more and more warnings about a wide variety of things. Perhaps I wasn't paying attention when I was younger, but it feels like warnings are coming at us from every direction and from every sector of life. We are warned about the threat level for our national security. That never used to happen. We are warned about fire risk and ozone levels and bacteria in the water and the temperature of the oceans and the mercury in our fish and transfats and so many other things that we never used to hear about. I also think I know one of the reasons why: human beings are not the sharpest species around. We do a lot of dumb things and then we like to blame others for our own stupidity, so many companies have gone to protecting themselves. They warn us which then frees them from litigation risk. Perhaps you have read some of the more amusing ones: on a package of nuts: package contains nuts; on a new set of soccer shin pads: Warning – shin pads cannot protect any part of the body they do not cover; on an electric router: Warning – this product is not intended to be used as a dental drill; and my personal favorite, on a Swedish chainsaw: Warning – do not try to stop chain with hands. You know there is a hand-less guy in Sweden somewhere in the midst of a lawsuit.

We get warnings all the time, but our problem is we tend to ignore them. As a resident of Florida, I have seen this first hand during hurricane season. We get warned so many times by all manner of forecasters and weather people that we tune them out, including when Jim Cantore is getting blown all over a nearby beach. We think that the warnings are not really for us. Most of us ignore them until the hurricane is right on top of us.

In my life, I have eaten a lot of peanut butter. I probably eat it three or four times a week for breakfast. Not long ago, I discovered a warning about contaminated peanut butter. Honestly, I didn't change my behavior one bit. In my mind, the contamination was going to be someone else's jar, not mine. We get so many warnings, that unless it's something unusual, we don't pay much attention to them.

This also has tremendous application in our spiritual lives. In case you've been living in a cave most of your life or you've never studied the Bible, God, out of His great love, is always trying to warn us. He does not want to see disaster come to us, plus He also knows well how we tend to behave, so we find him constantly say, "Look out!" Think about it: a warning is designed so that people can be ready for something that most likely will happen in their future. A warning is actually a means of protection. Thus, God is doing His best to prepare us for what this life will be like and to keep us out of trouble. We're warned about the powers of various temptations, about the true nature of our heart and its propensity for selfish decisions, about the greed of our world, about the violence that will increase as we get closer to the end, about how certain kinds of people will treat us, and about the trouble that we will most certainly encounter in this world, just to name a few. However, what do we do with those warnings? We tend to act like I did with the peanut butter or the hurricanes. We ignore them or start to feel immune to them. God is trying to keep us out of trouble by warning us, but I'm not so sure we're paying much attention. He wants us to be ready when we encounter various things, but because we are often not paying attention, we wind up being caught off guard, and the consequences of that can be devastating. The good news, however, is it doesn't have to be that way!

It is that idea that brings us to our text in **Genesis 41** where we meet a man who has received a warning from the Lord. As we study Joseph's experience and his response, I think there is much that we can learn as we try to understand what it means to live according to the Economy of God. Many of you know the story, but to refresh your memory, Joseph gets sold into slavery by his brothers when he is young, but by the grace of God, and largely because of his ability to interpret Pharaoh's dreams, Joseph rises to a place of prominence in Egypt. In fact, Pharaoh puts Joseph in charge of that entire country, and as he is preparing for that leadership role, he gets a warning.

In **verse 29**, it says, *"God has shown Pharaoh what he is about to do. Seven years of great abundance are coming throughout the land of Egypt, but seven years of famine will follow them. Then all the abundance in Egypt will be forgotten and a famine will ravage the land."* As a result of this warning, Joseph takes action. He plans. He enacts a plan to actively save enough resources to not only sustain his country, but to provide for many others around him during the years of famine that were to come. Then, as we would expect, events unfolded exactly as God had warned.

Understand, it was not unusual at that time for famines to occur. What was unusual was a famine of this magnitude.

Famines would occur in Egypt when there wasn't enough rain in the Sudan to flood the Nile, floods which would send nourishing water over northern Egypt. Famines would also occur if there was insufficient rain in Palestine or Syria. However, for rain to fail in all three of those places at the same time was extremely rare, and this made this famine one of the most severe and unusual that Egypt had ever seen. However, because Joseph had heeded God's warning, he was ready. Not only did Egypt endure the hardship, but Egypt thrived during a time when everyone else was ill-equipped, and she became an instrument of God in helping many others.

I don't want to draw too many parallels between Egypt then and what is happening in our economy now (the Great Recession), but we'd be foolish not to acknowledge some of them. We have enjoyed a time of almost unprecedented growth and prosperity in this country for the past twenty-five years, but right now, we are experiencing a unique convergence of circumstances that has led to one of the greatest economic crises in our history. Did we believe during those prosperous years that they would go on forever? Perhaps. Either that or we sought to remain blissfully ignorant so as to indulge our personal desires. We did this in spite of the numerous warnings that came from financial experts as well as people in our government. We didn't pay attention to the warnings that God gave us over and over that troubles and famines do come, that prosperity is not a right or a guarantee for any country or people. As a result, many of us were caught off guard. We weren't as ready as we should have been because we did not save. We did not store up. We did not prepare.

Let's look at some of what God's Word says to us about this:

Proverbs 21:20: *"In the house of the wise are stores of choice food and oil, but a foolish man devours all he has."*

Proverbs 30:24: *"Four things on earth are small, yet they are extremely wise; ants are creatures of little strength, yet they store up their food in the summer."*

Proverbs 13:22: *"A good man leaves an inheritance for his children's children."*

Ecclesiastes 5:14: *"I have seen . . . wealth hoarded so that when he has a son, there is nothing left for him."*

I could keep going, but I think you get my point. Over and over, God is warning us. He wants us to be ready for hardships that may come in the future, and He wants us to have a mind that thinks about the people who come after us. We need to be saving as a means of protecting and helping them.

Even so, when it comes to saving, we're not doing so hot. The news is not good. In 1984, the personal savings rate in this country was 10.8% of a person's gross income. That means that nearly 11% of what people made was being set aside for a later time. Nine years later, in 1993, it had dropped to 5.8%. By 2001, it was 1.8%, and in 2006, the savings rate hit an all-time low of -1%. In other words, we started spending more than we made. Those numbers paint a telling picture of the past twenty-five years. We have gradually been on a trajectory of self-interest, impatience, and growing discontent such that we have not been planning or preparing for the future nor for those who will come after us, but instead have spent all of our resources on us. I realize that many of you have saved, and in this economic crush, you have had to spend through that savings. That is not what I'm talking about. I'm talking about living in such a way that we ignore what God has said and focus only on our current wants and desires. If that's where we are, what might we learn from Joseph that will help us be better prepared for the future?

We Need to be Savers

First, while it should be obvious by now, *we need to be savers*. We need to be saving a portion of what we are making, setting it aside for the challenges that may come later and for those who will come after us. **Verse 49** says, *"Joseph stored up huge quantities of grain, like the sand of the sea..."* He knew that the period of abundance would not last and that he needed to set aside a portion of what God was providing.

Saving is a clear Biblical concept, and it is also part of the revealed nature of God. God has saved for us, so as His children, we are called to be ready and save for others. Paul writes in **Ephesians 1:13-14,** *"Having believed, you were marked in him with a seal, the promised Holy Spirit, who is a deposit guaranteeing our inheritance until the redemption of those who are God's possession – to the praise of His glory."* **1 Peter 1:4** says, *"He has given us new birth* *into a living hope through Jesus Christ...an inheritance that can never perish."*

Here is what God has done for you in Christ: In human time, He has made a deposit on your life that you will experience in full later. You have an inheritance in Jesus Christ. God has set aside something eternally for you. This concept is part of the nature of God, and if it's part of His nature and we are called to be shaped into the image of Christ, then saving and setting aside should be part of our nature as well. Matthew Henry writes, "We out to foresee the approaching period of the days both of our prosperity and of our opportunity, and therefore must not be secure in the enjoyment of our prosperity nor slothful in the improvement of our opportunity; years of plenty will end, therefore, whatever thy hands find to do, do it; and gather in gathering time." (Gospel of Matthew Commentary, Chapter 24) God warns us. He tells us that life has a way of changing, and He says, "Get ready. Store up. Save."

Saving is Based on Our Hope in God

Second, our ability to save *is based on our future hope in something, namely, our hope in God and in the lives of those He has entrusted to us.* Joseph planted and harvested that grain and took the time to create vehicles that could hold vast amounts because he had already seen the mighty hand of God at work in His life. He understood there was a purpose to His life that was greater than His desires, and there were people whom God had entrusted to Him who needed his care. If He didn't think God was faithful, he wouldn't do all that. If he didn't think God had a plan, he wouldn't go to the trouble. If he did not believe that he had a responsibility for those whom God had entrusted to him, he wouldn't do it, but he did all of it because he had an unswerving hope in what God will do in the future. If your life is all about you and you don't have any sense of God's power or plan, then why save? Why would you ready yourself for the future? You wouldn't. If you have no hope then you'll do nothing to plan. If you think the future is pointless, then you're going to run through everything you have today to try to numb that pain.

    About ten years ago, David Foster Wallace was widely viewed as the next great American novelist. His 1996 novel, *Infinite Jest*, was hailed by *Time* magazine as one of the 100 greatest novels of all time. Sadly, in 2008, he took his own life. A commencement address he gave in 2005 revealed the hopeless state of his heart. He said, "The traffic jams and crowded aisles and long checkout lines give me time to think, and if I don't make a conscious decision about how to think and what to pay attention to, I'm going to be pissed and miserable every time I have to food-shop because my natural default setting is the certainty that situations like that are really all about me, about my hungriness and my fatigue and my desire to get home, and it's going to seem, for all the world, like everybody else is just in my way, and who are all these people in my way? And look at how repulsive most of them are and how stupid and cow-like and dead-eyed and nonhuman they seem here in the check-out line…"

It's one of the saddest things I've ever read. He has nothing larger than himself to hope for in life so he can't even imagine getting past the check-out line at the grocery store, let alone a future in which God has purpose for his life. Our hope in God and His sovereign power is what compels us to be ready for that future.

Compelled by Love

Then, we are compelled *by the love we have for others and the responsibility we bear in their lives.* Joseph loved the people whom God had entrusted to him; thus, he was willing to go to great lengths to prepare and save for the future. What a gift he gave them. Do you remember what we read in Proverbs 13? A wise man saves for his children's children. God lays before us a multi-generational concept. Our things are not just about us but about those God has entrusted to us and what will happen to them long after we are gone. To save for those we may never meet may mean making sacrifices now, but what a gift and legacy we leave. Read these words of Elton Trueblood: "Man is so made that he cannot find genuine satisfaction unless his life is transcendent . . . it must transcend his own brief time in that he builds for the time when he is gone and thereby denies mortality." (As quoted in **The Beautiful Fight**, Gary Thomas, Chapter 9.)

If we don't care for those we love to the extent that we are willing to plan for their lives after we are gone, then we'll spend all we have on ourselves. My grandmother and my grandfather raised my dad on Long Island in New York during the Great Depression and the years that followed. They never had much, and long after my dad had moved away and after her husband had died, my grandmother still lived in that same little house and she still had very little. We would give her a new dress every year on her birthday, but those dresses rarely got worn because she was "saving them for a special occasion." She wore the same house dress day after day, rarely spending a dime on herself. Meanwhile, she was saving her money. You can imagine my shock when my dad called following my grandmother's death to tell me she had left me $10,000. I learned only later that my grandmother had been working a savings plan. She had been so careful in her spending all those years because she was taking every nickel and putting it in the stock market such that when she died, she had accumulated a tidy little sum.

It's hard to express the emotion I felt in that moment. I was in my first pastorate in Chattanooga, I had just had my first child, and that money was like manna falling from Heaven. I was overwhelmed by a deep sense of her love for me in knowing that all those years my grandmother had gone without, had laid aside her desires, in order to leave something to me and my sisters. Saving happens when we love and sacrifice for those who God has entrusted to us.

We Need to Have a Plan

Third, if we get to that place where we realize we need to do this; that is, we realize we need to save, then *we also need to have a plan.* Saving doesn't just happen. Just like giving, you have to plan to save. Sadly, the vast majority of people don't' do that. That's a tough one. And I'm not talking about getting a credit card that pays you 5% cash back on your purchases. Isn't that funny how we do that? We are enticed to sign up for credit cards that pay us a small amount of money when we buy things at an interest rate far larger than any percentage we're going to get back. In our minds, we think, "Hey, I'm making money while I'm spending." We think that's our savings plan! No. Let's go back and look at Joseph.

Verse 48 tells us, *"Joseph collected all the food produced in those seven years of abundance in Egypt and stored it in the cities."* While it's not readily evident on the surface, commentators on this text reveal that for Joseph to save that much grain, he had to come up with a means of storing it. He had to plan. He had to come up with storehouses so that the grain would not spoil in those seven years, and that's just what he did. So, let me ask you, beyond acknowledging that you need to save, do you have a plan to save? We have to do more than pay lip service to the idea if we are actually going to build up a reserve. I am amazed at the number of people who actually have no idea where their money is going. They get to the end of the month and what they know is they don't have much left, and they really can't tell you where it went. Friends, if God has entrusted us with His resources, don't you think we should do a better job of accounting for them? If we don't know where it's going, how can we plan to save some of it? We need to have a plan.

One of my favorite parts in Tolkien's epic *The Lord of the Rings* comes at the end of the Two Towers. Sam and Frodo are weary from carrying the darkness of the ring, and Frodo says, "I can't do this, Sam." He says, "I know. It's all wrong. We shouldn't even be here, but we are. It's like in the great stories, Mr. Frodo – full of darkness and danger they were. And sometimes you didn't want to know the end because how could the end be happy? But in the end, it's only a passing thing, this shadow. Even darkness must pass. A new day will come. And when sun shines, it will shine out the clearer. Those were the stories that stayed with you, that meant something, even if you were too small to understand why. But I think, Mr. Frodo, I do understand. Folk in those stories had lots of chances of turning back, only they didn't. They kept going, because they were holding on to something." Frodo says, "What are WE holding on to, Sam?" "That there's some good in this world, Mr. Frodo, and its worth fighting for."

I know for many, the shadows seem to be increasing. The darkness looms and grows in this time, but our hope is in the fact that we are caught up in the larger story of God—a future hope in which this darkness shall pass and the light of life will shine. So, we fight on. We work and we plan and we prepare and we save so that we will be as ready as we possibly can to be about the business of His Kingdom, all for His glory.

CHAPTER 8

PROSPERITY PERSPECTIVE

"I have learned to be content whatever the circumstances." (Philippians 4:11)

"I have made many millions, but they have brought me no happiness." (John D. Rockefeller)

There were three men who had been friends all their lives. They shared many of the same values and ideals about life, and they had each worked hard to become successful in their respective fields. As it so happened, these three men met and married women at about the same time, each woman coming from a different state.

The first man married a woman from Michigan, and as

was his belief, he told her she was to do the dishes and the house cleaning in the beautiful home he had provided. It took a few days, but on the third day he came home to find the house clean and the dishes put away. Now, the second friend married a woman from Iowa. They settled on a large piece of land with a huge home and nice cars. As was his belief, he told her she had to do all the cleaning, the dishes and the cooking. It took her some adjusting, but by the third day the man came home to find the house clean, the dishes put away, and a huge dinner on the table. Now, the third friend married a woman from Florida. He gave her many, many things, but told her that he expected her to clean the house, do the dishes, mow the lawn, wash the clothes and the cars, and cook hot meals three times a day. The first day, he didn't notice a change in his bride nor did he on the second day. However, on the third day, some of the swelling had gone down and he could now see out of his left eye, and his arm was healed enough so that he could fix himself a sandwich and load the dishwasher. I guess you could say she had a different perspective on the prosperity of her life and what was required of her to have it!

Without question, even as challenging as our economy is these days, we still live in the midst of great wealth and prosperity. We see it all around us. Actually, we all have some of it. However, there are many perspectives on the prosperity that we have, especially as it relates to our relationship with God. We hear so many things: everything from money is bad to God wants you to be wealthy and will make it happen if you just send money to the address on the screen below. One perspective often heard is loosely defined as the "prosperity gospel." That is the notion that God wants us to be financially wealthy, and if we are faithful in our giving, He will provide it.

Let me give you an example: George Adams lost his job at a tile factory in Ohio, and believing that his family needed to be part of Joel Osteen's church in Houston, he moved there. He believed Osteen's messages would lead him back to success. Inspired by the Osteen mantra that God desires to shower financial blessings on us in this life, he stormed into a Houston Ford dealership and demanded a job in sales and got it. (progressivevalues.org) He sold a truck on his fourth day, after which he said, "It's a new day God has given me. I'm on my way to a six-figure income. Once I get to six figures, we're going to buy our dream house: twenty-five acres, three bedrooms with a schoolhouse (they homeschooled). We want horses and ponies for the boys, so we'll have a horse barn, and a pond, and maybe some cattle. I'm dreaming big because all of heaven is dreaming big. Because I want to follow Jesus and do what He ordained, God wants to support us." For Mr. Adams, not only is God going to support him, but he feels that God's support will total six figures with land and horses. He and his pastor share that perspective, but is that idea well-grounded biblically? They are not alone, either.

There is a church in Texas which owns a $3.6 million dollar jet and a $6 million lakefront mansion in which the pastor and his family live. When asked about the opulence of such holdings for a church, the answer given was: "The Lord wanted us to have it. He wants to bless us." It is an interesting perspective on prosperity, indeed, one we see often here and one that is sweeping Latin America as well. So, in light of those two stories, what is your perspective on prosperity? As you think about what you have and what others have and how what you have compares to others, what is your perspective on prosperity, and does that perspective have anything to do with your relationship with God or His Word?

It is that idea that brings us to that Word, because it is the only way we can gain the proper perspective on anything. We come to a fairly well-known passage in Paul's letter to the Philippian church, chapter four, in which he is responding to a gift that the church has given him. In verse ten, he says, "*I rejoice greatly in the Lord that at last you have renewed your concern for me.*" That concern was expressed to Paul in the form of a financial offering that had been taken up by the church and given to him. As an itinerant preacher, Paul did not have a means of providing for himself. He depended on the gifts of others and many of those gifts came through the churches he served.

In Paul's writings, he never asked for assistance. He no doubt trusted in God's provision and therefore rejoiced in any gift that was given. Now, like most communities, including our own, Philippi was obsessed with material wealth. Thus, Paul used the opportunity of receiving this gift to also share a Godly perspective on his own prosperity. He says, in effect, "Thanks for the gift, but here's what you need to know about money and things. Here's a prosperity perspective." So, from Paul's life experience and the wisdom that he shares with this church, what might we learn about the concept of wealth and its impact on our relationship with God?

God is in the Business of Giving

First, let's be clear: *God is in the business of giving*. God wants to bless us. As Paul is explaining his views on worldly things, he says he can do everything because of what God gives him. I don't think I need to deliver a litany of ways God does that with you, but the cross of Christ would be a good place to start. God gives. God blesses. Jesus said in John 10:10, "*I came that you might have life and have it abundantly*." That does not mean that God wants us to be miserable in life. It means He wants to give. He wants to bless, and some of that blessing is going to be material and financial.

Isn't that how it works in our lives? It gives me joy to give things to my children. Out of my love for them and the joy I receive in giving to them, my inclination is to give them more than I should. Why would God be any different? He wants to bless us. It delights Him to do so. As a parent, I am also aware that giving my children things may also be detrimental to them. I am not going to give them everything they ask for because they lack the maturity to understand certain things. When my children were little, they would have been pleased if I had given them all the candy they wanted or let them ride their bicycles freely down the middle of the street. I did not allow it because it was not best for them. They, of course, did not grasp that at the time. They thought I was being rigid and unfair. They simply lacked the maturity to understand it, and when it comes to how God gives us gifts, we are in the same place. We lack the spiritual maturity to fully understand it. God knows us. Yes, He wants to give us things, but His giving is also governed by a love that wants only what is best for us, not what might harm us. His giving is motivated by a desire to shape our heart, not merely feed our personal desires.

Contentment

Second, as we appropriate God's blessings, some of which are material and financial, *the principle that we are to observe in dealing with them is contentment*. Paul writes in verse 11, *"I have learned to be content whatever the circumstances."* He says in verse 12, *"I have learned the secret of being content in any and every situation."* Hungry or full, rich or poor, Paul has learned to be content. This is a concept we have discussed several times in this book. We talked about how our discontent drives much of our impulsive spending. Our discontent makes us do things without seeking the counsel of others. Our discontent can cause our personal integrity to falter because we think the end justifies the means. And now, as we look at how to understand the whole dynamic of prosperity and plenty, God says the key is our contentment. So, let me ask you: Are you content with what you have right now? And, perhaps the harder question: If some of what you have was taken away, would you still be content? Some of you are facing that very thing. Well, let me be the first to answer. No, I'm not content with what I have right now. I want to tell you that I am, but I'm not. I want things. I covet things. I do. I'm human. However, I want to learn to be content, so how do I do that?

Our discontent begins with a false assumption or a false understanding. We think we are meant to have it all. We think we should lack nothing. That's certainly what our culture sells us. Our economy is built on our need to consume more, yet that is a false assumption. We don't necessarily need more. At no time has God promised you everything. In the garden before sin entered the world, Adam and Eve did not have it all. They could not eat the fruit from the tree in the middle of the garden. They were humans. They were not God. They had certain parameters around their lives. However, if we live with that false assumption, it naturally leads us to a sense of entitlement. We're supposed to have what we want, and if we don't have it then we're disappointed with life and discontented with our circumstances. No. You are entitled to nothing, but you are blessed by everything. Every good and perfect gift comes from the Lord; thus, we should be content and rejoice as Paul did.

While that sounds good, what's the problem with that? We base our contentment or lack of contentment on how our things compare to others. If it was just us, then we would look at what we have and say, "Thanks for the beans, Lord!"

However, as we're eating our beans, we look up and see our neighbor eating a big steak, and suddenly our beans don't look so good and our hearts are no longer grateful or content. That's called coveting. We covet what others have. Here's what we must understand: comparison is the biggest enemy of contentment. Comparison is what creates false rationalizations in our minds that allow us to justify expenditures we should not be making. We look at what others have and say, "Well, if they have that, then surely God wants me to have that." Jesus dealt with the disciples on this quite sternly.

In John 21:17ff, Jesus and Peter have a conversation about Peter's future life, a life that was going to be very painful and challenging. Then Peter sees John walking along, and says, "Lord, what about him?" Jesus has just revealed the very painful life that Peter would endure. As Peter mulls that over, I am sure he thought, "Well, I'll do what I have to do, but I wonder how that compares?" He sees John, and basically askes, "How does my future compare with his?" Jesus answers quite clearly in John 21:22 saying "What is that to you? You must follow me." I absolutely love the entire exchange. I love it because Peter is my representative. He does the same thing I do all the time. I am constantly comparing my life to others. I love it, too, because of Jesus' clear directive. Jesus has a plan for the world, and I am not privy to it. Therefore, if he is doing something in another's life, I have no idea what that is and I know nothing about that person's life, so every comparison will be inaccurate and wrong. My task is to keep my eyes focused on what Jesus is calling ME to do. As C.S. Lewis said, "To play well the scenes we are in concerns us much more than to guess about the scenes that follow it." (*The World's Last Night and Other Essays*, C.S. Lewis) In regard to our perspective on our money, this applies. We don't know about what is happening in the lives of others. That's another scene. We are to play well the scene WE are in, and be faithful to the Lord as we play it.

This is the case for all of us. Don't compare. Don't assess your life based on others. What God is doing in the lives of others around you is not your concern. Your concern is to follow the Lord in what He has ordained as the plan and purpose for you. If you compare what you have to others, you will never be content. However, there is an antidote. The antidote to discontentment is faithful generosity. The antidote to coveting what others have and comparing what you have to others is simple: Give. Give in accordance with God's commands and you'll see an amazing change in your heart. God wants to bless us. The principle for understanding those blessings is a life of contentment.

Having a Relationship With God

Third, *our prosperity, no matter how large or how small, will always be meaningless apart from a relationship with Jesus Christ.* Paul learned to be content in his plenty because He walked with the Lord. Your things will eat you alive unless you know Christ and know Him deeply. Solomon, one of the great kings of Israel, who by today's standards made $35 million a year, lived in a palace that took thirteen years to build and had 40,000 stalls full of horses. In looking back on his life, he said, "*Vanity of vanities, all is vanity, all is ceaseless striving after the wind*" (Ecclesiastes 12:8). In other words, no amount of money or things can ever bring you true happiness or meaning in life.

Have you ever noticed how frequently people who win the lottery wind up with broken lives? Some years ago, a man and a woman each won $17 million in a lottery drawing, and in only three years, each had died, one from liver poisoning stemming from alcoholism and the other from a drug overdose. It's not always the case, but it does happen frequently. Money won't make us happy, and when managed poorly, it can absolutely destroy us. As Warren Buffett said, "If you were a jerk before, you'll be a bigger jerk with a million dollars." Money can bring out the worst in us. It can't make us happy. Our happiness and satisfaction is grounded in our relationship with the Lord, who said, "*It is more blessed (happy) to give, than to receive.*" Without a relationship with God, your stuff may well ruin you.

Prosperity is Not a Right or a Guarantee in the Christian Life

Fourth, *prosperity is not a right or a guarantee in the Christian life*. Paul was one of the most faithful servants of the Lord and yet he said, "Look, my life has been both. I have had good times and I have had tough times." If there was such a thing as a "prosperity gospel"—some promise of God that He wanted us to have an abundance of material things—don't you think Paul or Peter or Job or Joseph or someone would have asked that question? Of course they would have, but they didn't. No such thing was understood. None of God's faithful disciples had such a view. Now, to be sure, some people will take verses like Philippians 4:19 which says, *"And my God will meet all your needs according to his glorious riches in Christ Jesus"* and use it to claim the right to financial riches for the Christian in this life. That is called prooftexting which is taking one verse out of Scripture and creating an entire doctrine around it without allowing the rest of Scripture to inform its understanding. If you spend five minutes on that text, you will know that the "riches" referred to are spiritual in nature, not financial. Those who walked with God did not claim riches. They claimed the opposite. They said things like "It is a privilege to suffer for the Gospel"; "In this world you will have trouble"; "The Lord gives and the Lord takes away, blessed be the name of the Lord."

God absolutely wants to bless us, but He also wants to shape us and teach us and train us. He wants to draw us into deeper dependence on Him. Make no mistake about it: you will go through periods when you will NOT be prosperous and some of you are in that period right now. If God never allowed such moments in our lives, how would He ever get our attention? How are we ever going to depend on Him if we always have everything we want and can depend on ourselves?

How are we ever going to grow beyond a shallow heart if we never encounter hardship? You can't and you won't; thus, as a gracious loving parent, God does NOT give us unfettered prosperity. You can't allow your financial position to be a barometer of God's love for you. It has nothing to do with that. Whatever your circumstances, God has allowed them for a reason and will use them to mold and shape your heart.

Having said that, we also have to ask the question: Is it wrong to be wealthy? How are we to view our prosperity or wealth if we have it? Are we supposed to feel guilty about it? There are some who would say you cannot be wealthy and be a sincere Christian at the same time, thus making poverty a spiritual virtue. Wrong. God does call some people to a life of poverty, but that does not make wealth wrong. Again in Ecclesiastes, Solomon says, *"If you get blessed, enjoy it, for it is the gift of God."* When you walk with God, you'll see your wealth for what it is: His blessing, and you'll work to allocate it faithfully. Make no mistake about it: it is challenging to be wealthy because wealth creates many temptations and distractions which is why God said it is harder for a wealthy person to enter the Kingdom of Heaven than for a camel to get through the eye of a needle. If you are prosperous, then you best sit down and do a hard analysis of your faithfulness. You may be sideways and not even know it, but at the same time, it's not wrong to have wealth. Don't look now, but the Bible is full of very faithful, very wealthy people. Being wealthy is not wrong. It's what we do with our wealth that makes that determination.

Martin Rinkart was born in a small German town in 1586. Though poor, he became a Lutheran minister just as the Thirty Years War began in that country, his home town of Eilenberg being the center of that conflict. Overrun with refugees, he could not feed or clothe all those in need; the suffering was overwhelming. Plagues swept the city, and Rinkart found himself often doing fifty funerals per day – per **day**. Such hardships lasted not one or two years, but thirty years. Twenty years into that thirty year struggle, he wrote a hymn:

> *Now thank we all our God with heart and hands and voices,*
> *Who wondrous things hath done, In whom His world rejoices;*
> *Who, from our mother's arms, Hath blessed us on our way*
> *With countless gifts of love, and still is ours today.*

Rinkart wrote those words from a heart contented in the Lord Jesus, rejoicing in His blessings, both large and small, and trusting in the Lord as He went about His calling. I believe that is the reality for all of us. We will likely never know the intensity of suffering that Rinkart experienced, but the Gospel we claim is one that can give us proper perspective on the grace of God and the riches of God. It is not a personal "road map" to financial means, but a trust in the provision of God and our call to fulfill His purposes through our lives. We are called by faith to joyfully receive His gifts, to be faithful, not comparing ourselves to others but walking humbly with the Lord. Make no mistake: in Christ, we are rich in all things. May our desire for worldly things be countered by the faithfulness of our giving to His Kingdom.

CHAPTER 9

LOOK UP!

"I will lift up my eyes to the hills..." (Psalm 121:1)

"I'm just thankful for everything, all the blessings in my life, trying to stay that way. I think that's the best way to start your day and finish your day. It keeps everything in perspective." (Tim Tebow)

One Friday night, my daughter Kaylee and I had a dinner date. We waited until about 7:30 p.m. to go out, so by the time we got to the restaurant there was a crowd of people waiting outside for a table. The hostess told us we could wait thirty minutes for a table, or we could sit at any open table in the bar. Naturally, being the great parent I am, I chose the table in the bar with the TV showing the Orlando Magic basketball game. We sat down and started looking at our menus when it became almost impossible NOT to overhear the conversation at the table just behind us. At that table were four young adults—two men and two women who were probably in their late 20's. I think it's safe to say they had been a bit overserved. They were very loud in what they were saying and also very animated. However, that's not what got my attention.

What got my attention was the subject matter: end of life issues. They were talking about what they would want done to them and for them in the event they were in a coma or had a terminal illness. They discussed euthanasia and whether they would take their own life if diagnosed with a terminal illness. I looked at Kaylee, and said, "This is interesting. Let's see if they mention God." Well, they didn't. They talked passionately about the end of their lives, but at no time did they ever mention God or the possibility that their lives would go on after this one. I was startled by this omission. From there, they proceeded to talk about obtaining peace in the Middle East and what they would each do if one of them were put in charge. Trust me, none of those four should be put in charge of anything.

As Kaylee and I sat there, I told her, "Let's do a little experiment in grace. I'm going to pay their bill, and then let's see how they react." This is actually something our family does from time to time, and it can be quite entertaining. We'll pick out a table, anonymously buy their meal, and then carefully watch what they do when they find out. It's a hoot. Initially, the people will look at the server in shock and disbelief. Some people start scanning the restaurant. Others try to protest and insist it is NOT true. People just do not get it. They cannot believe that the bill has been paid, and this group of four could not believe it, either.

Kaylee and I were facing the TV watching the game when the waitress came out to tell them. Their first reaction was to ask, "Who paid?" The waitress told them repeatedly that she could not reveal that information, but that someone had felt compelled to do it. With each refusal, the two women at the table became more and more upset. One of them said, "That's not right. Someone can't just buy my dinner without me knowing!" Honestly, she got mad about it. Then, the guys went in the other direction. One said, "You mean this entire meal cost us nothing? Well, then, let's go! It's a bottomless pit of drinks; let's order some more!" Unfortunately, the waitress had to tell them that the bill was now closed. We listened for a few more minutes, and then we got up and headed home.

On the way home, we both agreed that what we had witnessed was sad, but not surprising. They had no concept, no perception of anything eternal. They had no way of comprehending anything outside of themselves. Thus, when something good happened to them, something they did not deserve, something outside their ability to explain, instead of being grateful, they got mad and then tried to take advantage of it even more. Because they lacked perspective on anything eternal, they did not have the capacity to receive grace outside of themselves. It was a sad and yet powerfully revealing experiment, all on a date with my daughter.

As we move towards the conclusion of this book, it is this idea that may well be the key for us if we are ever going to adopt God's economy as our way of life. We need to honestly look at our perspective – our world view. Do we have a short-term earthly perspective on life and our things, or do we have a long-term eternal one? What God has revealed about His economy is a vastly different perspective than the one we are taught in this earthly life. We are much more prone to living in the here and now. We easily get caught up in the moment. We are largely about this life and about this life's comfort, so much so that we deny or mentally delay the hard, cold reality that this life DOES end. You are going to die, and when you think about that, do you really think this earthly life is all there is? What is your perspective on what you have now versus what you'll have after you die? I always shake my head when I hear about the kings and the wealthy of ancient Egypt. When they died, they were often buried in tombs with all of their treasure surrounding them in the hope that it would follow them into the afterlife. They thought they were going to need that treasure, but instead, thousands of years later, all we have is a bunch of mummies in tombs with gold all around them.

God is always trying to get us to think about this. He is always trying to change our perspective on this life, to impress upon us the brevity of life and the eternal nature of the next. Here are just a few examples:

Psalm 49:17: "*He will take nothing with him when he dies, his splendor will not descend with him."* (He's obviously going to the wrong place.)

Matthew 5:29: *"If your right hand causes you to sin, cut it off and throw it away. It is better for you to lose one part of your body than for your whole body to go into hell."*

Mark 10:21: *"Go, sell everything you have and give it to the poor and you will have treasure in heaven."*

James 1:9: *"But the one who is rich should take pride in his low position, because he will pass away like a wild flower."* You don't take it with you.

Jesus is always challenging us on how we look at things. He is constantly pushing us to have a view that looks towards Him and not at this life. "Look up!" He says, "Look up!"

It is that idea that brings us to our text in the eighth chapter of the gospel of Mark where we find Jesus pushing this question yet again. His ministry has been picking up steam. He is doing more and more, and the supernatural nature of what He is doing is generating more questions about His identity. People keep asking, "Who is this man?" In this chapter, we find the famous question that Jesus poses to His disciples when He asked, *"Who do you say that I am?"* This chapter also contains the account of the feeding of the four thousand and a brief dialogue with some of the religious leaders, including the Pharisees. Then we come to one of the first mentions of what is to come: Jesus talks about the cross. As He is discussing it, I want you to pay careful attention to the language He uses. It is the language of two worlds colliding. It is language that draws each of us to a fork in the road because it is the language of the world, the language of our culture. *It is the language of money.*

The translation in the NIV is not as strong as some others, but Jesus asks in verse 36, "*What good is it . . .?*"Or perhaps a closer reading of it would be "*What does it profit a man if he gains the whole world but forfeits, or loses, his soul? Or what could a person give in exchange for his soul?*" As Jesus is trying to communicate to the crowd, not just the disciples, He starts trying to explain two Kingdoms. There is the kingdom of this world and the Kingdom of God, and He wanted those gathered to know that they had a choice to make. In order to do that, He decides to speak in their language: the language of economy – commerce - money. Profits and losses. Gains and forfeitures. Deals and bargaining and negotiations.

Clearly, Jesus understood this was the language the people would understand. It was the language that the worldly-minded Pharisees understood, and make no mistake, it is our language as well. Do you think our world is a little caught up in profits and losses and forfeitures these days? Are we spending a lot of time listening to bargaining and negotiating about how this thing or that thing might be saved? You bet we are. It is the reality of recession. It worked that way then and it works that way today and Jesus understood that. He is, for all practical purposes, defining what it means to live in His economy and not our own, and we have to choose between them. Not choosing is also a choice.

So, from these powerful, economically-driven words of

Jesus, what do we learn about the choices we face in our future as we try to live as His disciples? It involves three things, and I'm going to take them in reverse order.

We Have to be Followers of Jesus Christ

First, if we want to live in the Economy of God, *we have to be followers of Jesus Christ.* This is the language of discipleship. During Jesus' time, if you were a disciple of someone, that meant you literally followed them around and applied their teaching to your life. You lived with them and according to their ways. In our increasingly individualistic present society, I am not sure we are very good at "following" anyone but ourselves. We just don't grasp the concept. There is a huge difference between showing up for worship, serving on a committee or going on a mission trip - and being a true disciple of Jesus Christ. We need to ask ourselves where we fall on that spectrum. Do we know the language of faith and the behavior of faith, or do we actually know the heart of faith and the heart of Christ? Further, we need to consider who is teaching us or exerting influence. Like it or not, we are all being influenced by someone or something. We all have teachers, so it's important for us to discern who and what they are.

Some people are followers of Warren Buffet, the megamillionaire investor. Whatever he writes or says, some people are going to read and listen. Others may follow Martha Stewart or Michelle Obama or Oprah Winfrey, lapping up their personal brand of wisdom and culture. Still others are followers of Bruce Springsteen, Taylor Swift or YoY o Ma, investing huge dollars in concerts and downloaded music. Maybe we don't go traveling all over the country, but we need to seriously ask ourselves, "Who am I following?" And if you say you are a follower of Jesus Christ then what are you doing that demonstrates that commitment? What are you doing to live according to His commands?

Part of me is tempted to stop there because it's much easier to leave it at that, but Jesus actually defines what following Him looks like. Following Him means two things, and this is where it gets challenging. This is where we arrive at the fork in the road—that choice—as to whether or not we really want to live according to His Economy. To follow Christ means a *denial of self and a daily carrying of our cross*. Most of you have heard those phrases or terms before, but let's spend a few moments on what they mean. To follow Christ, we must deny ourselves. This is directly opposite the teaching of the prosperity gospel. To deny yourself is to be more concerned about the Kingdom of God and less concerned about your own kingdom. It is to align your priorities, including your finances, in accordance with that perspective. It is not about what you want or desire, your ambitions or goals, but it is about living purely in God's will. You are always trying to discern how He wants to use you for His Kingdom purposes.

William Lane writes, "The central thought in self-denial is a disowning of any claim that may be urged by the self, a sustained willingness to say 'NO' to oneself in order to be able to say 'YES' to God. This involves a radical denunciation of all self-idolatry and of every attempt to establish one's own life in accordance with the dictates of self." (Lane, **Commentary on Mark**) Talk about the opposite of what we are taught in this life. In this culture, it is not the denial of self, but the celebration of self. And because we are not willing to deny ourselves for the sake of following Christ, we have evolved our theology into an easy-going spirituality in which God does not actually ask us to deny ourselves. Most have a view of God that allows them to do what they want because all God does is love. He demands nothing, least of all the surrender of your life to His purpose.

I know this is hard, and I know that we will never do this perfectly, least of all me. Yet, I remind you, if we don't, we have everything to lose. If you don't do this, what's at stake? Your life. If you don't deny yourself, in the end, you've gained nothing. Solomon, by all accounts one of the wealthiest men in the world, did that very thing. He denied himself nothing. Ecclesiastes 2:10 says, "*I denied myself nothing my eyes desired; I refused my heart no pleasure, yet when I surveyed all my hands had done and what I had toiled to achieve, everything was meaningless.*" He did it. Gold, silver, food, drink, women, music, knowledge—you name it, he had it, and it was meaningless. Been there, done that, and told you about it, but do we listen?

The Sultan of Brunei has a personal fortune of 22 billion dollars. He owns 5000 cars, a $233 million Boeing 747 filled with gold-plated furniture. He has solid gold toilets in his bathrooms. He has denied himself nothing, yet in the end, what will all of that really matter? His perspective is only of this earth, but God is trying to get us to look up. If we don't deny ourselves here, we run the risk of losing it all there, and in the end, here does not matter. Here is temporary. Here is nothing. So which is the wiser choice?

To follow Jesus, we must deny ourselves, and then we have to carry our cross. This is a vastly misunderstood phrase. When Jesus uttered these words, the cross was understood as one of the most reviled forms of death one could experience. To carry a beam of the cross on which you would be hung and killed was the most shameful and humiliating thing you could be asked to do, so to "carry our cross" does not mean some casual inconvenience in our life. James Brooks writes, "To take up the cross could only have been an admonition to martyrdom. The concept should not be cheapened by applying it to enduring some irritation or burden. Such a concept of discipleship is so radical that many contemporary Christians in the West have difficulty relating to it." (Brooks, **New American Commentary, Mark**) I would say so. To take up our cross is a further description of denying ourselves such that our lives are lived in the manner of Christ. We lay down our lives for others around us. And that is only possible insofar as we have been filled by Christ's love first. You can't lay down your life and deny yourself unless you first understand how Christ has done that for you.

You love and sacrifice because you have been loved and sacrificed for! Often, our first thought is, "Well, how much fun is that kind of life? I don't want that." Oh, yes, you do! The sweetness and joy of life in Christ is unmatched by anything this world could give. Bishop Hooper, the night before his own martyrdom, wrote "This life is sweet and this death is bitter, but eternal death is more bitter and eternal life is MORE sweet." (**Foxe's Book of Martyrs**, John Hooper) As a pastor, I have had many moments sitting at the bed of the dying, and they are sacred moments. I can promise you the joy I feel in ushering the faithful to the gates of Heaven is more profound than anything I could ever purchase in this life because in those moments nothing you could buy or acquire matters. It's meaningless. It doesn't count. The cross is everything and this life is nothing. That's what Jesus is trying to tell us. That's how Jesus is trying to get us to live. It is the true life—the abundant life—that we yearn for and that we only find when we take up His cross and commit our lives to His Kingdom.

Tony Campolo tells a great story about a conversation he had with a friend of his who was describing a funeral he attended. He said when the service was over and those gathered went to the graveyard for the burial, they were met by a large crane holding a brand new Cadillac in the air above the hole it would be buried in. As the pastor shared his final thoughts, the car was slowly lowered toward the ground, revealing the deceased man, sitting upright behind the wheel, clutching a solid gold steering wheel, surrounded by plush leather and solid wood trim. As the car slowly descended into the ground and those gathered sat in hushed silence, one man was heard to say, "Wow! Now that's living."

Sadly, I think that is our perspective at times. We think this world is all that matters, or at least that's how we act and live. I hope that can change. I pray that in the chapters of this book, you have learned something about what it means to live according to a different economy—a different system—such that our perspective on life is not about our things and our comfort and our stuff, but a surrendering of those things to the greater Kingdom of God and His call upon our lives to be used therein. The Economy of God is about becoming followers and disciples of Jesus, denying ourselves, laying down our lives and letting the cross become the ethic by which we live and make our choices. May God's Holy Spirit continue to teach us and convict us about this as we seek to follow Him!

CHAPTER 10

TIME FOR THE TALENT SHOW

"Now to each one the manifestation of the Spirit is given for the common good." (1 Corinthians 12:7)

"I have no special talent. I am only passionately curious." (Albert Einstein)

A look at the entertainment landscape shows that we are people who love to search for talent in others. Television shows like *American Idol, America's Got Talent, The Voice* and *The X Factor* have become wildly popular as they search from coast to coast for people who have talent. The reason we watch these shows is because we love being surprised when people step on stage that might appear unlikely to have talent and yet they wind up being fantastic. My favorite such moment was from *Britain's Got Talent*. A young man named Paul Potts stepped out on stage, and he was introduced as a "mobile phone salesman from South Wales." He had a paunch in his middle, did not appear to be in good shape, and when he opened his mouth you could see he had a number of crooked teeth. He told the interviewer that he had little confidence and had always struggled with low self-esteem. When he stepped up to the microphone he said he was going to sing opera. Well, Simon Cowell and Piers Morgan, two of the judges at the time, looked at each other and rolled their eyes, as if to say "There is no way this guy has the talent to do that." Well, you guessed it. He opened his mouth and sang what is known as the "greatest three minutes in Opera": a portion of Puccini's *Turandot* called "Nessun Dorma." It was glorious. He was phenomenal. People in the audience started going wild. Some of the women were crying. The entire crowd rose to their feet. It was just so amazingly unexpected and beautiful. They were affirming, "Hey, this guy's got talent!" and he went on to win the original season of that show and produce a best-selling CD.

As good a story as that is, the thought crossed my mind: What if I was on that show? Honestly, I would have nothing to offer. I can remember feeling like an outsider—like a failure of sorts—in grade school when we would have a talent show because I could never do anything. All these other kids could do all this stuff. I just sat there and wondered why I had no "talent." I can't sing or dance or play an instrument or juggle, so I would definitely not make it to Hollywood on *American Idol*!

Sadly, that is often how we decide to assign value to others in this culture. We assign value based on talent: whether someone can sing or write music or play an instrument; whether someone can dunk a basketball or hit a baseball or run fast or swim long distances; whether someone can act in movies or plays; whether someone can cook or make beautiful clothes. We look at those people and say, "Ah, you've got talent. We value you and will pay you handsomely to show us your talent." However, you never see someone on any of those shows come out and say, "Mr. Cowell, I am so excited to be here. You will see behind me I have brought my 9th grade algebra class. For my performance, I am going to teach algebra!"

Or you wheel out someone in a hospital bed and say, "Mr. Cowell, I am now going to put an IV in this man's arm and change his bandages because I am a very talented nurse!" Ratings would go down if you had tax accountants doing their work on stage because that's not what we consider talent. On and on we go, comparing ourselves to these cultural definitions, believing as I did that we don't measure up, or that we have to sit out because we're not qualified. Clearly, all of this begs the question: What or who defines talent? And if we discover that we actually have some of it, what are we supposed to do with it?

We find the answer to that question in the gospel of Matthew 25 as Jesus comes to teach one of His most famous parables, the parable of the talents. Keep in mind, as Jesus tells this parable, He has already entered Jerusalem in the last week of His life. He is very near the end. His betrayal, trial, suffering and cross will soon unfold, so He is teaching His disciples what the Kingdom of God is about. Imagine the urgency that Jesus must have felt in these moments as He is preparing His disciples. He is going to talk to them about the absolute most important matters. This is it! So, what is His subject matter?

He begins to talk about stewardship. He says this is a story about how a person ought to live in My Kingdom. Some of that involves money, but in this parable, our understanding of stewardship becomes something even larger than the normal context in which we hear that word. We will look at a broad understanding of what we mean when we talk about stewardship or this idea that we are "stewards" of God's resources. It's not JUST about money. Stewardship is the whole of life because all of life is given to us by God.

In Matthew 25, Jesus says there is an owner who gives three of his servants some "talents." A talent, as we find it used here, is not singing and dancing. A talent in Jesus' time was actually a sum of money. **It was a monetary unit that represented what a laborer might hope to earn in half a lifetime.** This man is not handing out small portions, but he is giving out small fortunes. Five talents would have been understood as an enormous sum that one could hardly spend in a lifetime. So you can start to see that this is not just a parable about money, but something larger.

Donald Hagner writes, "The parable sets the

responsibility of the servants in terms of money, but the symbolism points to something obviously more comprehensive." (***Word Biblical Commentary, Matthew***) The idea is this: God sovereignly chooses to pour certain gifts, abilities, and resources into our lives, and then He has an expectation that we will use them in a way that builds His Kingdom and glorifies His name. Therefore, let's examine these verses to learn how we might live in this Kingdom as we seek to be disciples of Jesus Christ.

The Absence of the Master

First, there is an important truth that often gets lost in this parable. The entire first half of this parable *takes place in the absence of the master.* Verse 14 tells us, *"Again, it will be like a man going on a journey."* The master is gone. In verse 19, we are told *"After a long time, the master of those servants returned and settled accounts with them."* What does this remind you of? The master leaves, and there is a long time between his departure and his return. Even so, the master gives his servants talents, and when he comes back he expects to see that they have been used faithfully and wisely. Friends, this is a picture of the departure and the second coming of Jesus. He (Jesus) is reminding His disciples, yet again, that He is about to go on a long journey. The master will be absent, but he says, "I want you to take what I have given to you and use it wisely." Consequently, what you see in the servants is urgency in their actions. Verse 16 says,

"They went at once…" There was no hesitation. They wanted to serve and please their master and be ready for his return.

In our Christian faith, I'm not sure we understand that urgency. The business of the Master is vitally important. He has entrusted us with these gifts and abilities, and we will have to give an account for what we did with them when He returns. What's more, this is actually about the Master's Kingdom, and there should be nothing more important to us than to please the Master by how we use His gifts towards that end. So, let me ask you: What are you doing to use your God-given gifts and abilities to build His Kingdom? Or, are you using those same gifts to build your own kingdom? Imagine for a second the Master coming back and asking for an accounting, and all you can say is that you took what He gave you and used it on yourself. We can no longer view the church as a place where we come to get what we want or need; it has to be more than that. We have to think missionally. We have to think about living on mission, out in the world stewarding what God has given us to bring His Kingdom to bear in our neighborhood, our families and our vocations. The Master is coming back, and we need to live with the urgency that knowledge brings. God's Kingdom work urgently matters.

No One is Exempt

Second, *no one is exempt*. No one gets to sit on the sideline. Every servant received something according to their ability. So, yes, in the Kingdom of God, some have more ability and thus are entrusted with more, but that does not minimize the significance of every person's role. Remember, just one talent was a fortune! Everyone has received an enormous amount to use! The Master's expectation was that every single servant would make a contribution to his Kingdom work. No one got to sit out because everyone was gifted.

Paul writes in 1 Corinthians 12 regarding the Holy Spirit as the giver of gifts in the Body of Christ. He writes in verse 7, *"Now to each one the manifestation of the Spirit is given for the common good."* The gifts and abilities God gives us are manifestations of His Spirit. They come from Him, and they are given for a very specific purpose. They are NOT given for your sole benefit. They are given for the COMMON GOOD. Friends, here is the good news: God has poured an enormous trust of gifts and abilities into your life. It is a manifestation of His Spirit, and He wants you to use them for the benefit of all. Further, he says these gifts are given to "each one." That's all of us. No one is excluded. I doubt anything frustrates God more than when He sees one of us wasting the very things He has given us, knowing how those gifts could be used!

One of my favorite movies is *Remember the Titans*. It is about the integration of a high school in Alexandria, VA, during the early 1970's. During one scene, two talented players, one black and one white, are forced by the coach to have a conversation with each other. Both have been frustrated by the entire situation, so neither has been working particularly hard.

They have not tried to help or encourage each other. The black player tells the white player he's not being honest, to which the white player responds, "Honesty? You want honesty? Honestly, I think you're nothing. Nothing but a pure waste of God-given talent. You don't listen to nobody…and every time you act that way you leave one of your teammates hanging out to dry." The black player then says, "Why should I give a hoot about you? You're a captain, right? You're supposed to lead this team, right? Well, honesty reflects leadership, captain."

There must be days when God looks down at us and thinks, "My goodness, what a pure waste of the talent I have given him, and when he lives that way, he leaves the rest of the body weaker and exposed." Going back to a sermon I preached one winter, we have become deeply narcissistic in our culture such that everything is about us. We have no sense of responsibility to a larger whole—to God's larger kingdom, to the community of people around us, or to our world—so we wind up thinking, "Why should I care about what's happening to that person?" The answer is because the Master has given you gifts that might change that person's life. There are things at work that are larger than you are, and that demands both your attention and response. It's our responsibility to care about others, and if we don't lead well, then we can't expect others to respond. They can't because they've never seen a model for life different from the current culture.

We can't be neutral. God wants all of us to be advancing the Kingdom. Why was the master upset with the servant who got the one talent and buried it? That servant wasn't the prodigal son, was he? He didn't go out and squander the master's gifts on himself. He wasn't flagrantly disobedient, so why was the master upset with him? He was upset because he stayed stuck in neutral; because his fear of losing the one talent caused him to do nothing. He didn't hurt the Kingdom, but he didn't build it either. He failed to trust that God would empower Him to fulfill his calling.

I wonder if that's where we are today. I wonder if we are a bit like that one-talent servant. We're not doing anything to hurt the Kingdom. We're nice people. We pay our bills on time and try to help our friends when they are in trouble. We come to church regularly and maybe serve on a committee or help with the youth, but are we doing anything to advance the Kingdom? Have we become like that one-talent guy, just burying what we have, or are we advancing God's Kingdom, boldly and faithfully using God's gifts for His glory? That's who I want to be! Our gifts are to be used for the common good, so friends, get in the game. Get off the sidelines. You can't be lukewarm. You're either for Him or against Him, but please don't bury what you have or use it solely for yourself. That's what sends the Master over the edge.

We Start From a Slightly Different Place

Finally, I think we will grow as stewards of life when *we start from a slightly different place*. We tend to think of stewardship in terms of what we are supposed to give, but this parable is actually about what we have received. It all begins with what God has given us. When we think and pray about all that God has poured into our lives, stewardship becomes about thanksgiving. Thanks and giving. Stewardship of life is about both. It's about thanks to God and it's about offering ourselves in joyful response. One leads to the other. So, let's reflect and think for a moment about what you have been given.

Too often, we get hung up on comparing ourselves with others or wondering why someone we know has five talents and we only have one. As I have said before, comparisons will eat you alive. Comparison robs you of your ability to be thankful because you think God has shortchanged you somehow. No! God has a unique and personal plan for you, so don't worry about the other guy. Your task is to take what God has given you and use those gifts such that they have the greatest impact on His Kingdom.

Further, you need to get beyond how the world defines talent. Don't look at a list of gifts and abilities as greater or lesser. I can stand up and preach in front of a lot of people each Sunday, but that does not mean I have a greater gift than the gifts of the guys in the control room who work hard at making me seen and heard. Without them, guess what? The Kingdom does not advance. So let me ask you about some gifts that commonly go overlooked: Are you a kind person? Do you have the sort of heart that feels empathy and compassion for the weak or the less fortunate or even for those who are downright mean? The Body of Christ desperately needs you.

Are you a friendly person? Do you find it natural to smile at someone and engage them even when they may appear shy or closed off? The Body of Christ desperately needs you. We need you to help others feel they belong.

Are you a discerning person? Do you have that internal gift that allows you to sense when there is something wrong with another person, someone who may be sad or sick or discouraged? We need your gifts.

Do you have the gift of unconditional service? Do you enjoy using your gifts to cook or clean or fix doors or mow lawns for the simple joy of what it brings to another person? Our Body needs you.

Do you have the gift of mercy? Do you have a heart that hurts where others hurt and one that wants to pray and care for those who suffer? I would love to have you visit people in hospitals or nursing homes. Our Body needs you.

Do you have a gift for strategy or organization? Can you see complex issues or situations and then imagine a path through them? Our Body needs you.

I could go on and on. We need to stop defining our understanding of "talent" so narrowly or exclusively. We need to stop believing that God may have short-changed us in comparison to others. He has poured a lot into your life. Talk to your friends. Talk to your spouse. Talk to those who know you. Talk to the leaders or pastors at your church. Ask them to help you discern what your gifts may be, and then exercise that gift for the advancement of the Kingdom of God. It all comes from God: your money, your abilities, your time, your intelligence. If it all comes from Him, then be faithful in how you use it, not merely for yourself, but to advance the Kingdom of God.

I love the old story about St. Francis of Assisi who was out hoeing his garden one day when a passerby stopped and asked him, "St. Francis, what would you do today if you knew that you would die tonight?" St. Francis replied, "Well, I would go right on hoeing my garden." In his mind, he was living his life in a way that he was ready for the Master's return. He was content that he was doing what God had called him to do with his gifts on any given day—to help grow food, in this instance, to feed the poor of his community—and if he knew the Master was coming back, he would continue to use those talents to maximize their benefit.

Friends, the Master has poured an abundance of personal, spiritual, and material gifts into your life. He's not here now, but He's coming back, and He has an expectation that we will all be using these for His Kingdom work. What are yours? Explore and ask and pray, then be faithful in your giving—your financial giving, your spiritual giving, your intellectual giving, your physical giving—such that when the Master returns, He will say to us, "*Well done, good and faithful servant. You have been faithful with a few things; I will put you in charge of many.*" To God be the glory.

CHAPTER 11

THE KINGS AND QUEENS OF PLANET EARTH

"Earth provides enough to satisfy every man's needs, but not every man's greed." (Mahatma Ghandi)

"For since the creation of the world God's invisible qualities--his eternal power and divine nature--have been clearly seen, being understood from what has been made, so that people are without excuse." (Romans 1:20)

When I was first employed as a pastor at Signal Mountain Presbyterian Church in 1991, I earned $38,500. Leigh was pregnant with John David, we had just bought a house for $87,000, and we had a 1985 Honda Accord. There was not a lot of room for extras in the budget; thus, we adopted the cash envelope system to help us live within our means. If we went to the haircut envelope and there was no cash, then we waited for that haircut. I had my share of shaggy-looking days. However, God provided for us in big and small ways, and one of the more memorable took place a few weeks before Christmas that year.

I was sitting in my office when my boss, Bill Dudley, called me and the other pastors into a conference room. When we arrived, we were met by one of the elders in the church who then introduced us to his tailor. He said that his tailor was there to take our measurements so he could start work on a custom suit for each of us. Clearly, this elder thought we all dressed pretty poorly. Now, I had never heard of a "custom suit" before. I thought that was something you had to put on when traveling internationally, but this tailor started showing us swatches of fabric and styles of lapel and varieties of vents in the back of the jacket, and I started to understand what was happening. To that point in my life, the only thing that I had ever had made just for me was the retainer made by my orthodontist. I was pretty excited.

The tailor came back three weeks later with a half-finished version of the suit. He fitted it and measured it again, and then after another three weeks, he came back with the finished product. I can tell you it was the best-fitting suit I have ever owned. It was amazing. Everything hit me just right. Every button, every crease, every bend. It was all perfect, and it was perfectly comfortable. Why? It had been made specifically for me. Anything that is made to fit us or that is made to our designs or specifications is always going to be better than something that is made in general. For that reason, many of you have specially fitted shoes because of the unique way your foot is formed or the way your arch is shaped. Some of you wear hard contact lenses that fit to the exact shape of your cornea. Some of you have golf clubs that are made to your height and swing path. One Christmas, our son Alex, who is 6'5", asked us for a desk chair that would fit him. He had grown weary of sitting in all the little desk chairs at the University of Florida. Thus, we got him an adjustable tall man's chair. We all love things that are designed specifically for us because, by definition, they work better and feel better. They were made with us in mind.

Well, there is something else that has been made with you uniquely in mind, and it is the planet that you live on. We don't spent much time thinking about this, but when you look at our text and then consider the science behind the elements of creation, we realize the absolute wonder of where we live and why it has been made as it is. In the first chapter of Genesis, God makes the earth, but Scripture tells us that it was made with specificity. God wanted certain kinds of animals and vegetation; He wanted dry ground and seas; He wanted a certain rhythm to light and darkness, and all of it was declared to be good. He then comes to His crowning achievement: the creation of human beings.

Unlike everything else, humans are made in the image of God. In a deeply spiritual sense, we are different from every other created being in that we have the capacity to be in relationship with the Creator. In verses 29 and 30, He gives the earth to the being He has created. Man is told to *"rule over it."* Therein we realize that as God was making everything, He was making it with us in mind. He knew He was going to give us this planet as our home, so He designed it with amazing specificity. It is designed to fit us and provide for us all that we will need, and science backs this up in a rather stunning fashion.

Consider the overwhelming odds against life ever occurring on this planet. Without getting too "scientific" here, to get a simple cell, there are millions of things that have to line up perfectly, all occurring at the same time. To sustain human life is even more profound. Frances Collins, the lead scientist in the mapping of the human genome, and other scientists have determined the odds that human life could ever occur would be like throwing 4 billion pennies into the air and having them all land heads-up. To look at this another way, it would be like having a blind man find a single marked grain of sand in the Sahara Desert three times in a row.

For us to live on this planet, the environment had to be meticulously and uniquely crafted just for us. It is absolutely custom made! Our culture does not like to hear it, but it points us to intelligent design. Perhaps you have heard of SETI (Search for Extra-Terrestrial Intelligence), a group searching the universe for signs of life by sending out signals while listening through an array of huge radio receivers for "organized" radio signals coming back. For these scientists, if a signal is random static, it is natural. If it is organized, however, it was undoubtedly sent by an intelligent source. For instance, the signal "2 – 2 – 4" (about 10 bytes of information) is considered to be intelligent. If they heard that coming back, it is not random. Obviously, someone with intelligence put those together.

By some stretch of logic, many of those same scientists say that a DNA molecule containing four billion bytes of perfectly arranged information did not come from a source of intelligence. They deduce that it just randomly "happened." Are you kidding? This world has been uniquely created for us by a Designer who knew exactly what we needed and what it would take for us to live according to His plan and purpose. It points us to the truth of Genesis 1.

So, if the planet has been custom made just so we could live here, what does that mean for us? How are we to understand that? Well, first, God created this planet for our enjoyment, our provision, and our care. Psalm 8 says: "*Lord, our Lord, how majestic is your name in all the earth! You have set your glory in the heavens…when I consider your heavens, the work of your fingers, the moon and the stars, which you have set in place, what is mankind that you are mindful of him?*" Paul affirms in Romans 1:20, "*For since the creation of the world God's invisible qualities – his eternal power and divine nature – have been clearly seen.*"

God is saying, "Look at what I made. Enjoy it. Praise Me

for it, for in it something of My power and glory and nature are revealed." There is a reason we get awestruck while looking at a sunset or the birth of a child. These incredible natural occurrences point us to the wonder and glory of God. He wants what He has made to be an outlet for us to enjoy and to praise Him! So, yes, appreciate mountains and beaches and vistas and sunsets and all of it. Love what God has made, for what He made points to His glory. What He has made is NOT God. We don't worship the earth or the creation; that is false, but we allow it to point us to the Creator!

God's Provision

Let's unpack what this means for us day to day. First, God has created His planet perfectly for us so that it might *provide for us what is necessary to live*, things like air and food and water. Verse 28 says, *"Be fruitful and increase in number; fill the earth and subdue it. Rule over the fish in the sea and the birds in the sky and over every living creature that moves along the ground."* God has given us breath. God has given us water. God has given us every source of food that we could need, but we cannot ignore how that same earth is providing those same elements for others. In other words, we cannot view our provision separately from the provision of our brothers and sisters who also live here. We have to see the earth's provision in a larger context, knowing that God's intention is to provide for all. And that's that good news: it can!

When our boys were in high school they used to love a reality show called *Man vs. Wild* starring a guy named Bear Grylls. This was the most macho guy in the world because he would have his crew drop him in some remote part of the world, and then he would have to survive until he could work his way back to civilization. What made the show amazing was what he knew about certain plants and where to find them, certain animals and what you could do with their meat or skin, how to find water and create fire. He was a walking billboard displaying that we can live on what the earth provides us. This planet is uniquely crafted so that we can live, but it also contains what is necessary to sustain our lives.

We Are to Care for the Planet

Second, and perhaps most importantly, *we are to care for this planet*. In other words, we cannot simply take our enjoyment and our provision at the neglect or destruction of the very gift that God has given us. In Genesis 1 and Psalm 8, God says we are to "rule over" the earth. Those words imply a royal or kingly understanding. It is as if we are the kings and queens of the earth and we have been called to rule over it. Solomon writes of this idea in Psalm 72:1: *"Endow the King with your justice, O God, the royal son with your righteousness. The mountains will bring prosperity to the people, the hills the fruit of righteousness. He will rule from sea to sea and from the River to the ends of the earth."*

God gives us the earth to rule and subdue, but we do so

as His assigned stewards. It is vital that we understand that. Who is the ultimate ruler? God. God is the Creator, and He has created this planet for us and then He says, "Look, I am going to make you the kings and queens of this planet, but my expectation is that you will care for it in the manner of royalty, with wisdom and care and compassion." We have been created to rule, but that rule is to be like our King's: compassionate and not exploitative. We govern and rule with God's entire Kingdom in mind, not just what it can or cannot do for one person. We are benevolent, compassionate, and faithful stewards of what God has entrusted to us.

Frankly, this is where it gets tough. This is where we have to ask ourselves hard questions about the exploitative nature of what we are doing to the planet. Yes, we can sit here and argue back and forth over global warming and the impact of how we live in our environment, but we cannot deny the way in which we live is gouging our planet. Christians, by definition, should care for the environment. How could we not? God made it, and what flows from His hand is good. How can we act as if it does not matter? There are consequences to how we live that we chalk up as necessary for our comforts, but at what cost to future generations? We cannot live in short-sighted fashion. Ignoring how we leave the planet for our children is not faithful stewardship. It is abdicating our responsibility as the kings and queens of this land, given to us by God to rule and subdue. So, yes, we subdue it. We make it give us what it has: coal and oil and minerals and wood and natural gas and all of its many other wonders, but we have to ensure that how we obtain them does not destroy the very land which has produced them, and when possible, that we replenish what we have taken.

Take a look at two things that are patently obvious: air and water quality. One of our most precious natural resources and one necessary for our lives is water, and yet we seem to be giving little attention to how we protect and maintain that resource. Right now in this country, 55% of our rivers, 1.2 million miles, are deemed of poor quality by the EPA because they are barely able to sustain aquatic life and would be suspect at best as a human water source primarily because of runoff contaminated by fertilizer. We're just being careless.

Air quality in China has gotten so bad that people in some cities can see no more than 200 feet in any direction. The World Health Organization has determined the measure for particulate matter in the air should not exceed 20 per cubic meter. China has said that they think a level of 200 is hazardous. Recently, by their own measure in Beijing, the number was 755. It was a number that far exceeded the range of any measurement chart. Respiratory illness soared as a result. These are painful and obvious problems, but we cannot ignore them simply to bow at the altar of progress or industry or personal comfort. We have been entrusted with the planet to rule and subdue, and how we engage in that bears witness to our understanding of God as Creator.

Viewing This Planet as Disposable

Finally, I think one of the most inherent reasons we are negligent in this is because we view this planet as disposable in some way, and that is a false understanding. This is not a disposable planet or a throw-away asset. There is this idea that we have gotten in our heads that we can use and abuse this planet in any way we want because one day we are all going to get whisked out of here and taken up to heaven. I liken it to the way my children live in their rooms. They are natural disaster areas, but they know they can walk out into a well-kept den with a nice television, so they just keep living that way. They always know they have the option of leaving their room. It is an immature understanding of what God has given to us and His call upon us in regard to its future use. This planet is not going anywhere. As God demonstrates again and again, He is going to redeem and restore and renew what He has made.

When the day of salvation comes, not only will we be restored and resurrected in glorified form, but so will this earth. Imagine that for a second. Isaiah 65:17-25 reads: *"Behold, I will create new heavens and a new earth. The former things will not be remembered, nor will they come to mind. But be glad and rejoice forever in what I will create…"*

Revelation 21:1 says, *"Then I saw the new heaven and the new earth, for the first heaven and the first earth had passed away and there was no longer any sea…and I heard a loud voice from the throne saying, 'Now the dwelling of God is with men, and he will live with them. They will be his people and God himself will be with them, and be their God. There will be no more death or mourning or crying or pain, for the old order of things has passed away."*

Does that sound like the earth is disposable? Heavens, no! God says in the end, He is going to re-create the heavens and earth. He is going to redeem and restore this planet. It will not be like the old one, but a redeemed one. In the same way, you and I will not be the same in our glorified form. We will be recognizable, and so will the earth. Not only that, but this becomes God's dwelling place. In the end, we all come here. Heaven comes down. God comes here and Heaven and earth merge into one. Now, can I explain that to you? No. But the reality of what happens in the end should inform how we view what happens here.

Maybe the best description of what I am talking about comes from C.S. Lewis in the seventh and final book of *The Chronicles of Narnia, The Last Battle*. It is, I suppose, his book of Revelation, his view of what happens at the end of all things. Narnia, the great land created by Aslan, is destroyed. The children mourn the loss deeply even though they continue to journey with Aslan towards what he calls his "country" or what would appear to be heaven; but then, it starts to look familiar to them. They start to recognize landmarks and places. What transpires at that moment reflects the biblical revelation of the New Earth. Lewis writes:

"But how can it be?" said Peter. "For Aslan

told us older ones that we should never return to Narnia, and here we are."

"Yes," said Eustace. "And we saw it all destroyed and the sun put out."

"And it's all so different," said Lucy.

"The Eagle is right," said the Lord Digory. "Listen, Peter. When Aslan said you could never go back to Narnia, he meant the Narnia you were thinking of. But that was not the real Narnia. That had a beginning and an end. It was only a shadow or a copy of the real Narnia, which has always been here and always will be here: just as our own world, England and all, is only a shadow or copy of something in Aslan's real world. You need not mourn over Narnia, Lucy. All of the old Narnia that mattered, all the dear creatures, have been drawn into the real Narnia through the Door. And of course it is different, as different as a real thing is from a shadow or as waking life is from a dream."

The difference between the old Narnia and the new Narnia was like that. The new one was a deeper country: every rock and flower and blade of grass looked as if it meant more. I can't describe it any better than that: if you ever get there, you will know what I mean.

It was the unicorn who summed up what

everyone was feeling. He stamped his right fore hoof on the ground and neighed and then cried: "I have come home at last! This is my real country! I belong here. This is the land I have been looking for all my life, though I never knew it til now. The reason why we loved the old Narnia is that it sometimes looked a little like this."

The good news of the gospel is that this earth is our future home—not exactly this, but a far grander and more majestic version. It is our real country, and for that reason, I take delight in knowing that one day I will see all its wonders. I will see the Grand Canyon and the Swiss Alps and the great coral reef. I will see the beauty of Niagara Falls and the wonders of the outback. It will all be here. We will see it and recognize it, but it will be strangely different. Brighter somehow. Complete and whole. It will be God's home as He comes to dwell with us. Let's be the Kings and Queens of this planet in the manner God intended us to be, and that is as faithful stewards, wise and compassionate, understanding that one day we will come back here to live eternally; thus, we care for our home and what flows from the benevolent and good hand of our Creator.

CHAPTER 12

PROTECT THIS HOUSE

"So that he might present the church to himself in splendor, without spot or wrinkle or any such thing, that she might be holy and without blemish." (Ephesians 5:27)

"I believe that one reason why the church of God at this present moment has so little influence over the world is because the world has so much influence over the church." (Charles Spurgeon)

I am not a handy person, period. I am probably the least handy person you know. I would like to be handy because I think being able to fix things or build things would be a huge asset, but that is not part of my gift set. For that reason, it will not surprise you to know that I have only been involved in building two houses in my life. The first was a Habitat for Humanity house in Chattanooga that our church had taken on as part of a one-week "blitz build." Everyone in the church signed up for time slots, and the idea was that you would complete the house in one week.

When my day came, and I went over to the house and found that the frame had gone up along with most of the wiring, and now it was time to put on the siding. You need to know that when you put on siding, you have to layer it so that one piece fits over the next and so on until you have covered the entire wall. Well, the foreman sets me up with a stack of siding, a hammer and a box of nails, shows me what to do, and leaves. Not good. I go to work, doing it exactly the way he said, but by the time I got the tenth piece on, I realized it was curving up and to the right. As I realize my mistake, the woman who was to occupy the house came by along with the foreman. He said, "David, I'm sorry, but you're going to have to take all that down and start over." I felt deeply embarrassed that I had messed up this woman's house. She was going to live there, and here I was doing shoddy work on it.

The second house was the one I worked on two summers ago at Mission Emmanuel in the Dominican Republic. We were sent out into the village of Cielo to help build cinder block homes instead of the sheet metal structures that many people lived in. In strong winds, those homes were easily destroyed, so the need for more substantial housing was tremendous. Each day, we would break into teams and go to home sites where we would mix concrete, lay block, or a host of other tasks in building these houses.

I must say that my experience on this house was far more rewarding. I was working on a wall, but I was not working by myself. I had many others around me, including the project foreman. Just like that Habitat House, the future inhabitants of that house were there, working right alongside of us. It was hot, dirty, hard work, but over the course of the day, I put up four rows of cinder block for what would be the back wall of this family's house. When I started working on it, it was at my knees and when I finished it was at my nose.

When it came time to go, the foreman came over to inspect what I had done, and he told me, "Good job." Even the owner looked pleased. I'm telling you, it was one of my proudest moments. I loved that wall. I took pictures of that wall. I showed those pictures to anyone who would look. I texted Leigh and said, "Honey, look, I built this wall." I felt like Tom Hanks in *Cast Away* when he made fire. "I, David Swanson, have made this wall!" However, that was not even the best part. The best part was stepping away to see the whole of the work that everyone had done, because while I had been working on my wall, ten others had been working on other sections, and by the end of three days, a house literally rose out of the ground, a home where a man and his wife and their children would live, a place that would protect them when it rained and shelter them when the wind blew.

I'll never forget that because it was, for me, a perfect

picture of what the church should be. I don't mean in the sense that our church was down there serving, but I mean in the way we, as the sons and daughters of God, are called to build His House—His Church. We each have different roles to play and different gifts. We each get an assignment so to speak, a section to work on, and while we're doing that, others are serving in other areas. It's not always easy. Far from it. Sometimes it's hard and exhausting and messy. However, before too long, we step back and a community of faith has literally grown right before our eyes: a community of faith built on a foundation centered in Jesus Christ and His Word; a spiritual home where people can go to be fed and nurtured and loved; a place where people can seek shelter during the storms of life; a home to which they belong. I'm not sure there's a better feeling in the world than to have invested in such a place—to have worked and served shoulder to shoulder with others—and then to step back and see what God has grown, what God has created through those efforts. There's just nothing quite like it. I think that is exactly what Paul is talking about in 1 Corinthians 3.

    Paul is writing this letter to the Corinthian church, and he is talking to them about how they are building it, or rather, what a poor job they are doing of building it. He says in verse 10, *"By the grace God has given me, I laid a foundation as an expert builder, and someone else is building on it, but each one should be careful how he builds."* We have been talking about this idea of stewardship - that it is a concept that means far more than money. It is about how we take care of things that have been entrusted to us by God. Just as Paul tells the people at Corinth, God is telling us today: the foundation for this church has been laid, and now others, namely, you and me, are called to keep building it. However, we have to *be careful* how we build on it. In other words, it's our turn. We are stewards of this church. God has built it over the years and now to each one of us, He says, "Here. I want you to take this and tend her and care for her and build her." I wonder, today, are we ready for that? Are you ready for that in the churches you serve? As we grow and mature in Christ, I am confident we will be.

Similar to our culture today, the church in Corinth existed in the midst of an elitist, religiously plural, intellectually pompous, generally arrogant community. Corinth was a booming cultural center, and as a result, she had a rather high opinion of herself. That arrogance also filtered into the church's life. They had accused Paul of not giving them enough of the Holy Spirit and threatened to follow other teachers. They had implied that they were, somehow, better or higher than other churches, but Paul quickly deals with that. He tells them in chapter one to quit boasting in themselves and to realize who they were before Christ found them. He tells them they need to be humble. He tells them to stop acting like a child as if the world revolved around them and to start acting like a disciple of Christ where their lives were committed to serving Christ. He essentially tells them to grow up. He then builds on that by specifically addressing the nature of the Corinthian Church, the community of those who are in Christ. As we think about the community that is First Presbyterian Church, with all the opportunities and challenges that are before us, there is much that we can learn and that we need to learn from Paul as he teaches us about our responsibility as the stewards of Christ's Church.

The Foundation is Jesus Christ

First, *the foundation is and always will be Jesus Christ.* Paul says in verse 11, *"For no one can lay any foundation other than the one already laid, which is Jesus Christ. If any man builds on this foundation using (other things), his work will be shown for what it is…the Day will bring it to light."* Paul says, "Look, the foundation of the Church is and always will be Jesus Christ, and if anyone tries to change that or build the Church in some other way, then it will be shown for what it is because the light of life will come to shine on it."

I have been so proud of our church in this last year because we have stood firm on that foundation. The reason we put up the cross in front of the Clayton Building is to remind us of the day in January 2012 when we said we were going to protect the foundation on which this church was built. We staked our future on our core belief in the authority of Scripture and the Lordship of Jesus Christ. That was awesome! Even so, here's the thing: We are still called to be stewards of this community of faith and, specifically, to protect the foundation on which she is built as others will surely try to compromise that truth in years to come. It's bound to happen.

Without question, the culture is trying to erode the foundations of the church and those put in place by Jesus Christ. In the next ten years, as our culture devolves, more and more pressure will be put on the Church to conform. And more and more pressure will be put on you, as disciples of Jesus Christ, to do the same. God has said quite clearly, if you try to build my church on anything other than Jesus, as verse 13 says, that work will be *"revealed with fire."* If the foundation is not true, then the walls will crack and the church will weaken and die. That is why cathedrals lay empty in Western Europe. They changed the spiritual foundation and the walls crumbled. We have a great challenge before us and a great opportunity. As the emptiness of our devolving culture becomes more and more pronounced, people will search for something on which they can stand and that something will be found in Christ's Church. We must not and we cannot compromise on that foundation or twenty-five years from now, you will find on this corner a renovated theater or office space, not a church.

Never Think of the Church as a Building

Second, we can *never allow ourselves to think of the church as a building, but as the covenant community of faith* formed when we come together. Paul says in verse 16, *"Don't you know that you yourselves are God's temple and that God's Spirit dwells in you?"* It's semi-rhetorical. Don't you know this? Have you forgotten this?

It's as if he is saying, "Come on, people, clue in here. God lives among you." You're His Church. You're His People. You – plural. God dwells wherever His people come to form communities of faith, and those communities are His divinely created dwellings found in particular places through which He comes to reveal Himself to the world.

Those communities are called churches. Churches are not buildings, but they are communities of people gathered in particular places where God comes to dwell. That's who we are. So, if this community is where God dwells, should we not care what it looks like, how it functions, what it says to those who come to visit, what it says to the person who actually lives here? In the same way that I wanted to build a good house for that family in the Dominican Republic, we should also earnestly desire to make the "Spiritual House" of our heavenly Father, this Church, everything He wants it to be. We should put our heart and soul and sweat and energy and resources and love into this place. If this is our Father's House, we cannot do otherwise.

And therein lays the problem. God has entrusted His Church—His House—to us, but we don't really see it that way. We function more like visitors than we do stewards. We don't sense the God-given responsibility that is before us. When I was in high school, I had a good friend who was not exactly one of my parent's favorite people. He had a rather lax attitude about many things and did not seem to care much about others. In my boyhood home, our front door was framed by two full length panes of stained glass that were my mother's absolute pride and joy. She loved those windows. One day my friend and I were outside throwing the football and he threw a wild pass right through one of those stained glass windows. Glass was everywhere. Some pieces were just hanging, dangling, and my mom was absolutely crushed. I was crushed. I could see the tears welling in her eyes, and my friend rather glibly said, "I'm sorry, Mrs. Swanson, but it's just glass. I'm sure you can get that fixed up like new." That's it. His perspective on my mother's house was just like our perspective of the church. He was only a visitor. He came and enjoyed the look and the view and the benefits, but he wasn't a steward of that house. My Mom was. She had worked on that house and had tirelessly helped craft and care for those windows. Oh that our attitude towards the church would be that of my mother's for our house that day.

I wonder as we think about our church, are we just visitors here, or are we stewards? I can tell you that the answer to that question is determined by our love for the owner. Brennan Manning, a well-known author and spiritual director, wrote, "Leadership in the church is not entrusted to successful fund-raisers, brilliant biblical scholars, administrative geniuses, or spellbinding preachers (though these assets may be helpful), but to those who have been laid waste by a consuming passion for Christ—passionate men and women for whom privilege and power are trivial compared to knowing and loving Jesus." (**Abba's Child**, Brennan Manning) What really matters is whether or not we have a consuming passion to know and love Jesus Christ, and when we do, we will naturally love and build and protect the house in which He dwells, the very Church for which He died. If we don't, then we won't pay it much mind at all because we are just visiting. It's not ours. We don't live here. This community is where God comes to dwell, and our love for Him compels us to treat it as if it were our own—to build it and love it and protect it as a faithful steward does for the owner.

God is Serious About This

Third and finally, *God is absolutely serious about this.* God loves His House. God loves His Church. Paul says in verse 17, *"If anyone destroys God's temple, God will destroy him; for God's temple is sacred and you are that temple."* God says, "The place where I come to dwell is sacred; it is holy, and if anyone sees it as anything less than that, if anyone does anything to hurt it or destroy it, then I will deal with them and it will be harsh because this matters to Me." God has set apart the church as sacred and holy. This is God's house and He WILL protect it.

One of my favorite jobs as a pastor is officiating at weddings. I get to stand at the head of the aisle 15 or 20 times a year. I have seen a lot of brides, and I can tell you that I am already trying to figure out how to get through it when that bride is my daughter. In that holiest of moments, as she stands at the head of the aisle, I will be a complete and utter mess, but can you imagine my rage if someone came and ruined that moment? What if someone jumped up with a protest sign or someone ran in the back of the building and threw something on her dress or ran up and knocked her down? I would probably have to go to jail for what I might do.

That's what God is saying here. This church, this community, is where God lives. It is His bride, and He is very, very serious about how we take care of it. He is very, very serious about how we take care of her. She is not to be slandered or maligned or ignored. This is a house that is not to fall into disrepair. This is the dwelling place of God through which He will reveal Himself to the world. He is the world's only hope; therefore, what are we each called to be and to do for His dwelling place? Yes, we all want our earthly dwellings to be a message to the world about who we are and our success in this world, but our houses, our empires, our kingdoms will all one day disappear. Let us aspire to something greater—something eternal. Let us invest in building the house of God, His Church.

Another one of my favorite images or symbols for the church came in a 2001 movie that starred Kevin Kline and Kristen Scott Thomas called *Life As A House*. It is the story of a lonely, divorced architect recently diagnosed with terminal cancer. When his estranged, drug-using son comes to live with him for the summer, the man decides that he wants to finally build the house of his dreams on the lot he has that overlooks the ocean. It is a fairly simple house on a small lot, but the house becomes a character in the movie. The house becomes a community project. As the man grows weaker, more and more people get involved in the project, and day after day, as people come to the house and invest in the house, they find purpose and community and healing and love. Lives get transformed. The man's ex-wife comes to help, and slowly, they reconcile their past. Eventually, she brings her new husband, a marriage rife with its own problems, and the two of them experience healing. The disconnected family next door realizes, once again, that they are a family, that they love and value each other. And the man finds a sweet and tender reconciliation with his son. The man dies just before the house is finished, but his son takes over and finishes the project. People come from all over to help having heard the story and wanting to be part of its power. Finally, when the movie ends, the house is offered to the family of a poor girl, paralyzed in a car accident many years earlier by the architect's drunken father, the house serving in the end as yet another instrument of reconciliation.

From the first time I saw that movie, I have always thought of that house as a church; for the church is far more than a place, but rather a character, a living thing, a bride that we all come to be part of and invest in and build and serve. As we do, as we come to love and serve the house—God's house—we find that we are miraculously and mysteriously transformed by the process. We are reconciled and forgiven and healed. We find meaning and purpose. We find relationships that transcend the pettiness of this life. We find hope. We find love. But if we never come, if we never serve, if we never invest, then the house is never built and we never have the privilege of experiencing that joy, that reconciliation, that hope. Our life is a house—this house: His community of faith. May we love and cherish her—and serve her—as we once again claim our foundation and our center at the cross of Jesus Christ. Amen.

Made in the USA
Columbia, SC
18 January 2019